On The Road to Peace
(Insight into Schizophrenia)

By: Linda Edmunds and Andrea Nelson

Copyright © 2010 by Linda Edmunds and Andrea Nelson

On the Road to Peace
(Insight into Schizophrenia)
by Linda Edmunds and Andrea Nelson

Printed in the United States of America

ISBN 9781609579302

All rights reserved solely by the author. The author guarantees all contents are original and do not infringe upon the legal rights of any other person or work. No part of this book may be reproduced in any form without the permission of the author. The views expressed in this book are not necessarily those of the publisher.

Unless otherwise indicated, Bible quotations are taken from The New King James Version. Copyright © 1994 by Thomas Nelson.

www.xulonpress.com

Dedication

I dedicate this book to my husband Tom, who graciously gave me the opportunity to follow God's leading...

Linda

I dedicate this book to my Dad, who never stopped loving me, my Mom, who never stopped praying for me and my Sister, who never gave up on me...

Andrea

When He, the Spirit of truth, has come, He will guide you into all truth. John 16:13

Chapter One

The Connection

linda

It has been a year now since Andrea moved in with my husband and me. It's 1:45 a.m. and I can't sleep. I really should watch my caffeine intake. As I peek into her room and watch her sleep peacefully, I am overcome with emotion. Her beautiful long blond hair lies softly on the pillow. Her breathing is unlabored and her face looks almost angelic as the dim light from outside finds its way through the cracks in the blinds. In just a few weeks, Andrea will be twenty-nine years old, and for the first time in her life, she understands who she is and why life has been, and always will be, a struggle for her. Andrea has a brain disease called *Paranoid Schizophrenia*.

Our story began just twenty-two months ago. So much has happened in such a short time. I have learned more about mental illness, and myself, than I thought possible. I recall when Roselyn Carter was our First Lady and choose mental illness as her "cause" thinking what an odd issue to choose. Lady Bird Johnson's passion was fighting the war on poverty. Pat Nixon's was the spirit of volunteer service, and Betty Ford's was equal rights for women, all of which I understood. I assumed Mrs. Carter was referring to depression and depression was something you had when you were dissatisfied with your life. Being a content person most of my life, my thoughts on the subject were very shallow. Get a grip and be happy with what the Lord has done for you. I would find myself getting an attitude when I would hear of pleads of insanity in our courts. Well, God was going to educate me in a way I never imagined, and in a way He does best.... by experience.

It was a warm September morning. As I looked out my office window at the clear sky, I couldn't help thinking how blessed I am. Three of my four kids had graduated from well-known Christian colleges, living on their own, working on their careers. My oldest son, Jonathan was engaged to a beautiful Christian woman and was to be married in four months. My son Mark had been dating a wonderful woman that he had met while attending Wheaton College, and it was only a matter of time before another announcement of betrothal would be made. My third child Laura Lee was living with her college roommates, experiencing life in the windy city of Chicago before coming back to California. Suzanne, my youngest, was in her third year at a prestigious state college on a full scholarship.

My husband Tom and I had recently sold our home and given away most of our possessions. Tom, following God's leading, had applied, and was accepted, at a local law school. We moved to an apartment just blocks away. It was just the two of us, in one apartment, with one car, living off my income. We were like newlyweds, madly in love, starting on a new adventure together. Life was relatively simple and unencumbered.

The sound of the phone ringing startled me and put my daydreaming to a halt.

"Hi Mom."

It was Suzanne. Right away I detected some anxiety in her voice. The cheerfulness I counted on from my youngest daughter was missing.

"What's wrong sweetheart?"

"Mom, do you remember Andrea, my counselor at Rawhide Ranch? She called me last night. She is sick and dying of AIDS, and we need to help her."

I vaguely remembered her counselor, having only met her once or twice. It had been years since Suzanne had gone to the horse camp. At the time, Suzanne was eleven and Andrea had just graduated high school. They had written and talked on the phone often the first year. I recalled Andrea picking Suzanne up from school once and taking her out for ice cream. It had been at least ten years since Suzanne and Andrea had communicated.

"Mom, she got involved with drugs and contracted AIDS."

"Why is she contacting you, honey, and how did she get your number at college?"

"I have no idea," replied Suzanne obviously concerned.

Suzanne told me about the phone call. The first thing that was odd was the timing. Andrea had called at 12:45 in the morning. Luckily, Suzanne was up studying for a test. After the initial courtesy chat, Suzanne asked her reason for calling. Andrea said she remembered Suzanne as a cool kid, who was close to God, and before daylight, she thought she was going to meet her Maker and was scared.

As Andrea's story unfolded, Suzanne was moved. That morning the girls spent four hours on the phone sharing, reading, and praying.

"Mom, Andrea is dying and she doesn't have anyone to pray with her and see her through this. I need to be there for her. Would you do me a favor and get a Bible to her?"

I told Suzanne I would.

Andrea's apartment was in a huge, low-income housing complex. Not wanting to intrude, I decided to leave the Bible by the front door with a note. The note simply said, "From your friend Suzanne."

The next day Suzanne called and said that Andrea had received the Bible and requested my work phone number. I gave my daughter permission to give Andrea my work number. The next morning Andrea called me. Her voice was childlike, yet very articulate in what she had to say. She was very gracious and thanked me for the Bible. I work in a teaching hospital that has a well-known AIDS clinic. I asked Andrea if she was familiar with the clinic and she said yes. I offered if she was ever at the clinic to give me a call and we would do lunch. It is one of those offers that you know is right, but you secretly hope the person never takes you up on it. I had done my part.

After my last parental lecture about limiting the phone calls and getting back to her studies, Suzanne didn't talk much about Andrea. I assumed the issue was resolved. What I did not know was that she was still calling Suzanne in the early morning hours.

Suzanne wanted to be a friend, but was becoming overwhelmed with Andrea's problems. Andrea had contracted AIDS while doing drugs in high school. A man from Andrea's church, old enough to be her father, had given her the drugs in exchange for sex. However, now that she was drug free, he still was in her life demanding the sex. He would show up at her apartment as often as three times a week. Andrea asked Suzanne never to call her on weekends or on Wednesday nights for fear he would be there. She said he was a powerful man, not only in his church, but also in the community.

Andrea was obviously very afraid of this man, but going to the authorities was out of the question. His influence in the community intimidated her. She had already tangled with the law and didn't feel her word against his would make a difference. Suzanne could not understand why Andrea could not go to her parents with her problems. She told Suzanne that she was adopted and had never really bonded with them. She loved them, but had only limited contact. Andrea admitted that she had very few friends because of the stigma attached to her illness. She also shared that the AIDS virus had entered her brain and she suffered periodically from dementia, which also scared people away.

Andrea's problems were more than Suzanne could imagine. Suzanne was only twenty years old and had lived a relatively sheltered life. She knew only love and acceptance from her family. Suzanne was very social and well liked, surrounded by good solid friends. Nevertheless, she was determined to be there for Andrea if only to be a listening ear.

Even though Suzanne was hearing from Andrea on a regular basis, it had been weeks since I had heard from Andrea. I figured she had taken my advice and contacted her parents for support. Andrea was the last person on my mind the day she called.

"Hey Linda, what's up?"

"Hi Andrea, how you doing?"

She said she had an appointment at one of our clinics and was taking me up on my lunch offer. I had brought some cottage cheese and an apple from home, which was going to be the extent of my lunch that day. I had a deadline to meet and I wasn't going to leave my office until it was done. Well, I did invite her to look me up if she was ever at the Medical Center. I had to stick to my word.

The phone rang and Andrea said she was in the hospital cafeteria. I immediately headed downstairs to meet her.

After looking around for a number of minutes I spotted someone with her head down on the table, face covered.

"Andrea?" I asked hesitantly.

Slowly her face appeared. She was very pale; her lips were cracked, and bleeding. It was obvious that this young woman was very dehydrated.

Without greeting me she said, "Can we get out of here? It is too noisy and it is hurting my ears."

I offered her some lunch before leaving, but she refused. She said she hadn't eaten for days because she had no appetite. I suggested we go outside where it would be quiet and private. We sat on a bench in a patio area. As she started to chat, I took that opportunity to make an assessment. Other than her pallor and cracked lips, she didn't look ill. She was about my height, 5'4, and weighed approximately 135 pounds. She had a pretty face; however, she was squinting her eyes and grimacing. Periodically she would stare out in space, giving the impression that something was distracting her.

I made mention of the necklace hanging on her neck with the initials MWS.

"Oh, that's for Michael W. Smith. I am sure you have heard of him. He is the most talented musician I know. I have all his albums on tape and some on CDs. On his latest one, "Live The Life," he wrote a song about me. I met him at a bookstore when he was promoting his new CD during his San Diego Tour."

Andrea seemed to come alive as she talked about her idol. I already knew a little about him. He is a well-known Christian artist who draws the attention of the younger generation. My kids have a couple of his CDs and I was familiar with a few of his more popular songs. I had gotten the impression from Suzanne that Andrea had not been living the life of a Christian for years, yet she enjoyed music that talked about faith and trust in God. I found this provocative.

"Well, tell me about this song he wrote about you." I suggested.

"The title of the song is, **Don't Give Up.** The words go: *Don't give up, Andrea, you got the whole world at your feet... Just keep on, holding on...this is where you need to be...*

I listened as she enthusiastically sang a few bars. If what she was saying was true, I could see why she was so excited. I tried to remember if I had heard the song.

An hour had gone by and I told Andrea that I really needed to get back to my office. We parted and started walking in opposite directions. After a few steps, I was compelled to turn around. Sadness came over me as I watched her walk away. Her oversized clothing made her look very vulnerable and pitiful. I had noticed that she had on two T-shirts under her jacket. Since the temperature was around 80 degrees, I found it odd. Then I had to remember she was very sick and staying warm usually was a problem when ill.

As I walked back to my office, I tried to shake the image. I had much work to do that afternoon and I couldn't afford to be distracted. In addition, I had no reason to believe I would see her again. She did tell me that she had parents who lived in the same town and an older sister, who lived a hundred miles away. I encouraged her to contact them and allow them the opportunity to support her during this difficult time.

Two hours had gone by and I was deep into my work when I received a phone call from Andrea. A very frightened voice came over the line.

"Linda, the nurse just called me and wants me to check into the hospital. She says my wet reading is low. I don't want to go into the hospital. I hate hospitals. It's like the roach motel... once you check in, you never check out."

I could tell she was verging on hysteria. I tried to assure her that being in the hospital wasn't so bad. If her physician thought it would be best, maybe she should consider his recommendation. She asked me if she had looked okay earlier that day. I could tell she was frantic and wanted my reassurance. I told her I could not assess how she was doing, as it was the first time we had met. Andrea was adamant that she was not going to check into the hospital and die like many of her friends who had AIDS. I prayed with her and said I would continue to pray throughout the day in hopes that she would make the right decision.

The day was flying by too quickly and I wasn't even close to finishing my report. After my brief phone conversation with Andrea, I was not only distracted, but also found myself feeling anxious and unsettled. I decided to at least look at the schedule of the day's clinic to see whose care Andrea was under. To my surprise, there was no listing for an Andrea Nelson, and adding to my bewilderment, she was not even registered as a patient in our healthcare system.

andrea

It's always easy for me to wake up in the morning when I have a great day planned. Today I am going to the Wild Animal Park with my friends from Kenesis. Kenesis is the day treatment center I attend four days a week. It is a program designed to help those who have a mental illness. My mental illness is schizophrenia; not just schizophrenia, but *paranoid* schizophrenia, the most devastating of all mental illnesses. It is not an easy label to carry around with you, but I am learning to *"grow where I have been planted."*

I will start my story with my friend Madeline. Throughout the years I stayed in contact with Madeline, one of my counselors from Outward Bound. Outward Bound is a program for troubled kids that my parents sent me on, the summer after my junior year of high school. I'll share more about that experience later. After Outward Bound, Madeline had become a psych nurse in a hospital. She lived in Seattle. Being in another State made it easy for me to talk to her. She had to have known that I had serious problems and maybe that is why she always made herself available to me when I called. Sometimes I would call a couple times a month and then wait for months before calling again. If she knew I had a mental illness, she never let on. When I would share with her some of my antics, she would tease me and say that I had "delightful deviant tendencies."

One day I mentioned to Madeline that I was once a counselor myself. It was at a Christian horse camp one summer. I shared with her about one camper whom I had connected with, just like she and I had connected. It saddened me that my friend and I had lost touch with each other. Suzanne was a strong Christian and encouraged me right after I accepted Jesus into my life. I often wondered what became of her. I thought it was so cool that Madeline and I remained friends and wished that Suzanne and I had stayed in touch. Madeline suggested I give Suzanne a call and see what she was up to. She told me that she was thrilled to hear from me once in a while and understood where I was coming from.

I still had Suzanne's phone number in my phone book, so one evening I decided to give her a call. When I called I got a recording stating that the number had been changed. I quickly wrote down the new number. I called and a woman answered. I assumed it was Suzanne's mom. I remembered meeting her mom once but could not picture her in my mind. I asked if Suzanne was home. Her mom said no, that Suzanne was away at college. I could hardly believe it. Little Suzanne was in college. I asked if she could give me the number where I could reach Suzanne. I could tell immediately that she did not want to give me her daughter's phone number. She started asking me questions. She wanted to know the reason for my call and if she could take a message. When I didn't answer right away, she asked my name. All I wanted was Suzanne's phone number and this lady was asking way too many questions. So I said I did not want to leave a message and hung up.

I thought about it for a few days, and decided to try again. Now that I was prepared for all the questions, I wouldn't get so flustered. This time a man answered and when I asked for Suzanne's phone number, he gave it to me without the third degree.

I didn't call Suzanne right away. I think I waited a week. Too many things were happening in my head and I got distracted. Finally one night, while alone in my apartment, I decided to call Suzanne. I really don't recall much of the conversation. I do remember that I had been drinking. My roommate and her daughter had gone out of town for a few days and I was having a hard time being by myself. At that time in my life, I would start drinking if my problems got overwhelming.

I vaguely recall Suzanne praying with me over the phone and asking me something about a Bible. When the Bible mysteriously arrived at my door less than a week later, I immediately knew it was from Suzanne. I called Suzanne and she told me that she had called her mom and asked her mom to get it for me as a gift. I thanked Suzanne, and thought I should also thank her mom for taking the time to pick it out and deliver it to me.

Suzanne said her mom started work early and therefore went to bed early. I think she was afraid I would call her mom during the hours I had made a habit of calling her. When I asked for her mom's work number she said she would call her mom and see if it was ok to give out. Suzanne definitely was a chip off the old block. I didn't know what the big deal was with these women in giving out phone numbers. Anyway, next time we talked Suzanne gave me her mom's work number.

The following day I called her mom and thanked her for delivering the Bible. Linda was very kind and said if I was ever down at the hospital, to give her a call and she would treat me to lunch.

About a month later I had an appointment down at the Medical Center. I called Suzanne's mom the day before my appointment and she suggested that I call her after I saw the doctor and we would meet for lunch.

When I was done with my appointment. I went into the cafeteria to dial her number on one of the hospital phones. By this time it was close to noon, and the cafeteria was extremely loud and overwhelming. My ears had become extremely sensitive. I just figured it was part of my illness.

Linda answered promptly with her professional, and now familiar greeting, "Reproductive Medicine. This is Linda Edmunds."

"Hey, I'm here," I said. "I'm down in the cafeteria."

"Okay Andrea, I'll be right down. Give me a clue as to what you look like so I can find you," she said.

"I'm the only kid here, and I'm wearing a Denver Bronco's hat," I replied.

After hanging up, I went to a small section of the cafeteria, which was off to the side of the main dining room. I tried to get comfortable in my new surroundings and waited for her. I felt sure she would be there quickly, but still the noise in the café along with the noise in my head was a lot for me to contend with. To try to get some peace, I lay my head on the table and tried to cover it with my arms.

What was probably just a few minutes seemed like hours to me. The Voices in my head were competing with the noises around me. I finally heard a soft outside voice gently call my name.

"Andrea, Andrea, is that you?"

I looked up and saw an attractive woman, my height, small frame, in her forties, dressed in a tailored green suit. I was a little taken back because she was not at all what I had imagined. I was expecting someone much older, and much more motherly looking. However it didn't take me more than a few seconds to see the compassion in her eyes. When she spoke, she had a gentle voice that soothed me. I immediately relaxed.

She offered to buy me lunch, but I declined because the café was just too loud. She could see I was uncomfortable and suggested we find a quiet place outside the hospital and talk. As we proceeded outside, I dutifully followed her like a lost puppy that had found its mommy. For some reason, I felt safe with her.

We sat down on a bench near some trees. We both attempted to get acquainted. She wasn't pushy, for which I was thankful. I really didn't want to volunteer any more information than necessary.

I don't remember much about what we talked about, only that I eagerly boasted about my recent meeting with the musical artist, Michael W. Smith. It was one thing I was confident to discuss. It wasn't a depressing subject and if anybody could talk about 'Smitty,' it was I.

Although I felt comfortable with Linda, I was still having some problems with the Voices and I could see the Demons up in the corners of the sky watching me. It was a little preoccupying to say the least, so when Linda said she needed to get back to work, I was grateful to be on my way home.

...If anyone sees his brother in need, but has no pity on him, how could the Lord God be in him? I John 3:17

Chapter Two

The Involvement

linda

Fall had arrived and life was just the way I liked it...quiet. I was anticipating a relaxing evening in front of the television and an early to bed agenda. Tom was a prisoner in the second bedroom working on a paper. Law school was proving to be a challenge. At fifty, he found himself needing twice the amount of time than his classmates to do the homework. He would joke about the kids coming to class with sand on their feet due to early morning surfing excursions or red eyes due to heavy partying the night before. The reality of his lack of youth was constantly hitting him between the eyes.

This particular night I did exactly what I had planned. After dinner I sat myself down in front of the television and ended the evening with a warm bath. It seemed like I was only asleep for a few minutes, when Tom gently nudged me on the shoulder.

"Honey, Andrea is on the phone and insists on talking to you." The look on his face told me this was not going to be a simple phone call.

"Hi Andrea, what's going on?" Struggling to focus my eyes on the clock on my nightstand, I noticed it was 10:45 p.m. I had been asleep at least an hour and a half.

"I am confused and scared. I am not sure where I am," said a frightened voice on the other end.

"What do your surroundings look like?"

"I am in front of a big store and everything is so loud, and the lights are so bright."

"Andrea, you have no idea where you are?"

"No."

Still half asleep, I was struggling to think. Ok, Linda, think... think.

"Andrea, tell me the last thing you remember."

"I was heading down to my appointment at the clinic, near where you work. They would not see me because I was late."

After asking a number of questions about her surroundings, I was pretty sure I knew her location. She was at a pay phone at Ralph's Market, a grocery store a few blocks from the hospital. I told her I would be there shortly.

It took me less time than I thought to throw on some jeans and a sweatshirt. I had told Andrea to stay by the pay phone and not move.

As I arrived, I could see her standing by the phone near the entrance of the store. She obviously did not recognize me as I approached. She jumped back acting very guarded. She looked at me as if I had something in my hand and was about to hit her with it. She was light on her toes and ready to duck.

"Andrea, it's me, Linda." I tried to calm her down and get her to sit down and relax.

She was like a cat on a hot tin roof. Had she been drinking? I couldn't tell. Was she on drugs? I had no way of knowing. Was it truly the AIDS virus that was attacking her brain and making her act so strange?

I asked her if she would let me take her to the hospital. She adamantly refused. I asked if I could call a friend to come for her. I got the same response, no. I asked if I might call her mother. She said no again, each time seeming more agitated. Then I asked her how I could help. I had run out of suggestions.

"Stay with me," she replied in a childlike manner.

Well, I had no intentions of spending the night in the parking lot of Ralph's Market, and I let her know it. Bringing her back to my apartment, not knowing what was wrong with her, was also out of the question.

While talking to her, she kept jumping around, very guarded as if someone was about to get her. Her eyes kept shifting away, looking for something. She said she had her car but forgot where she parked it. She was not in any condition to drive so the fact she had lost it was fine with me.

I was getting nowhere with her. She seemed to be getting worse. She would switch from being very jumpy to falling on the ground as if she had passed out. She would talk to me in a childlike manner almost begging for my help and then the next minute, yelling at me as if I was going to harm her.

Next to the grocery store was a jewelry store with a large picture window. Andrea jumped back full force into the glass. I thought for sure the window would break and she would set off the alarm. During one of her yelling modes, she told me to get lost. I knew I was in over my head and I had done everything possible to help her that evening. So before she changed her mind, I jumped in my car and went home. As I walked in the door, there was Tom holding the phone towards me, smiling as if to say, guess who?

"What do you want, Andrea? I can't help you unless you tell me what you want me to do."

"Please come back," said a pitiful voice, "I'm afraid, I don't want to be here alone." She immediately changed her tone and with a childlike excitement she informed me that she found her car.

I told her she had two choices. I would bring a blanket and a pillow and she could sleep in her car, or she could allow me to take her home. She said she would allow me to take her home. Therefore, I was back on the road again. As I approached the parking lot, I spotted her sitting in a 1988 Jeep Cherokee, with the door open and her legs dangling out. I rolled down my window.

"Get in before I change my mind." I said firmly.

She gave me a big smile and looked relieved to see me. I watched as she reached over and grabbed a security club and locked it on the steering wheel. She then locked the door and went around the other side to make sure the passenger side was locked. It fascinated me that someone so "out of her mind," was acting so responsible. It didn't make sense. As she jumped in my car, I noticed that she had some items with her. In one hand she had a small baggie, with Halloween pictures on it, filled with medicine bottles. The other arm held a yellow teddy bear and blanket very close to her chest.

As she got into my car she looked over at me and smiled. What a beautiful smile she had! At that moment, I said a quick prayer and we were on our way. I knew the drive to her apartment was at least twenty miles. I just wanted to get her home safely and then me home safely.

The ride was going ok. Very little talking was going on, which was fine with me.

Ten minutes into the ride, she looked at me and asked, "Where are we going?"

"I am taking you home Andrea."

All of a sudden, the car lit up. At first, I didn't realize what was happening. I looked over at Andrea and I could see her fiddling with the seat belt. Then I realized the car light was on because she had opened the car door. She was trying to jump out of the car! I was going at least sixty down the freeway. Before I knew it, I was grabbing her arm with my right hand and trying to drive and stay in my lane with the other.

I was able to keep her in the car, which to this day, I know was because of God's intervention. Andrea is a very strong young woman. For three years she worked as a loader for UPS. She could pick up over 100 lbs. without breaking a sweat. My one hundred and twenty pounds was no match for her.

I was desperately trying to keep her in the car while I was looking for the nearest off ramp. In order to calm her down I yelled, "Ok, ok, I won't take you home."

That seem to relax her for the moment and then she spotted the HOSPITAL sign. The ramp I had chosen was coincidentally near a hospital.

"Oh no you don't...you are not taking me to the hospital!" she shouted.

This time she did jump out, but I had already pulled into a gas station and was coming to a stop. Andrea fell out of the car and rolled a few yards from my car before ending face down on the ground. I was at my wits end.

"Lord, I hope you are in on this one, because I do not have a clue what is going on."

"Andrea, please come back over to the car. You left all your belongings. I have your teddy bear and blanket."

That worked. She got up and came over to the car. "Andrea, why are you so afraid? You said you wanted me to take you home. That is what I would like to do. I do not intend to take you to a hospital. Please get in the car and let me take you home." Reluctantly she got into the car.

"May I now take you home? You are tired and I think you would feel better if you were home in your own bed."

Even if she didn't feel better being home in her own bed, I certainly was going to feel better with her home and me in my own bed.

She agreed, as she put her seat belt back on. I noticed she was holding her blanket and stuffed teddy bear very tightly with both arms. We were back on the road again. This time I thought we'd better talk, so I tried to engage in conversation about how she remembered Suzanne. I figured if I kept the conversation light and continuous, she would relax.

We had been traveling and talking when she looked over at me and asked, "Where are you taking me?"

Oh no....not again. "Andrea, we agreed that the best place for you now is home."

Again the car light went on and the door was opening as she was trying to take her seat belt off. It was much easier for me to pull over this time because I had decided to drive in the far right lane more slowly. Just prior to the car coming to a complete stop, Andrea jumped out. She ran off and this time I could not see her. It was very dark and a lot of brush grew beside the road. I got out and started calling for her. I couldn't believe the predicament I was in: one o'clock in the morning, on the side of the road, cold and tired and yelling for a person to get back into my car, a person I hardly knew. Once again I found myself praying.

"God, please bring her back and help me get her home." Just then I heard some noise. As I looked in the direction of the noise, I strained my eyes to see a body lying in the brush.

"Andrea, get up and get into the car." I said it so firmly I think it took her by surprise. She did get into the car and I told her the next time she jumped out, I would drive off and leave her. Then she would be alone with nowhere to go.

We arrived at the housing development; however, I did not recall the actual complex and apartment number.

"Andrea, which building is yours?" I asked.

She looked at me surprised and said, "You can't take me there. He is there!"

"Who's there?"

"He's there."

I assumed that "He" was the man that had been abusing her for years.

"Look what he has done to me!" Andrea pulled her left coat sleeve down her arm and lifted her T-shirt sleeve up to the shoulder line, showing me a well-healed large scar.

"Look here." Andrea threw her leg up towards the dashboard of the car, pulled up her jeans just above her ankle and revealed another large scar not yet healed. Now I really didn't know what to do. If he really was there I did not want to see him and most importantly, I did not want him to see me. I wasn't sure what I should do. I just couldn't leave her, or could I?

Just then, she said she felt sick. Well the topper on the evening would be if she vomited in my new car. I insisted she get out of the car. As she was getting out, I noticed that she still had her teddy bear and blanket, but missing the baggie with Halloween pictures.

"Andrea, where is the baggie with your mediations?"

She shrugged her shoulders, as if to say I don't know.

I looked everywhere. I looked underneath the seats and all around my little Honda Civic. I remembered seeing it in the car the first time we stopped. What about the second stop? Just then, I recalled hearing something that could have been her medicine bottles fall out of the car. At the time, I thought it was a beer can that she kicked as she stumbled out of the car. It must have been her medicine hitting the ground. Great, I thought, we have to go back to our last stop. I did not know what medications she was taking, but I knew it was something she needed. And by the way she was acting, I assumed she needed to take something soon. So I told her to get into the car, we needed to go back to our last stop.

As soon as I was on the freeway, I noticed that my gas gauge was on empty. What now! Andrea told me the next gas station was about three miles down the road. As I pulled into the gas station Andrea jumped out and started pumping. Soon we were back in the car, in search of a baggie with medicine. I made it clear that once we found the medicine, I was driving her back to Ralph's Market and leaving her at her car. I suggested she sleep until she was able to drive home. I was tired and was calling it quits. She was on her own.

I heard Andrea mumbled something about me getting on her nerves. I couldn't help but comment.

"Sweetie, it wasn't too long into this adventure tonight, I found myself with only one nerve left, and right now you are standing on it. So don't push me."

It wasn't hard to find the area I had stopped. There were some definite landmarks. However, finding the bag of medication was another story.

As both of us were looking around the ground, I knew finding the baggie was slim. It was dark and the brush was thick. Just then I noticed a few feet away an orange object. I found the baggie! The moon had lit up the orange pumpkin picture on the decorative Halloween bag.

Once back on the road. Andrea seemed to be relaxed and accept the idea of me bringing her back to her car. During the ride back to Ralph's Market she became very quiet and I noticed that her eyes were shut. I figured she must be tired. I certainly was.

I sensed something strange happening. I looked over at Andrea and noticed that her arms and legs had gotten very stiff. Her fingers were clinched. Just then I looked at her face and to my horror, I realized she was having a seizure. Oh God, now what do I do? I knew that if I took her to an emergency room she would freak out. I had promised her just hours earlier that I would not take her to the hospital. Besides, do you take people to the hospital when they have seizures? Andrea did tell me that she had seizures all the time and they were no big deal. She didn't mention going to the hospital or requiring a physician's care.

For whatever odd reason, I turned the radio on. Maybe I wanted to escape the quiet. Softly the lyrics came through the radio speakers. "Just keep your eyes on Jesus...." keep your eyes on Jesus. Ok, that is what I will do. As I drove, I prayed.

As we were entering the parking lot of the supermarket where the evening had started, I glanced at Andrea. She had opened her eyes and I could see her body relaxing.

The first thing I wanted to do was go to a pay phone and call Tom. I wanted him to know that I was ok. I was sure he was worried. As I got out of the car, so did Andrea. I told her to go get into her car. She threw herself down on the ground face down and would not move. After trying to persuade her for a few minutes, I gave up and said I was going to go make my phone call.

As I was on the phone to Tom, I saw a fire truck come into the lot. I immediately had a sick feeling that their arrival had something to do with my new friend. I told Tom I needed to go and I hoped to be home shortly.

As I started walking towards my car, I could see Andrea was no longer lying on the ground where I had left her. I looked in the direction of the fire truck. I could see Andrea sitting on a curb talking to the paramedics. As I got closer I could hear the firefighter asking Andrea if she needed medical assistance. She was shaking her head no. They asked her a few simple questions, such as, who is the President of United States, in which she answered Hillary Clinton and giggled. One of the other firemen looked at me and asked if I knew the young lady. I whispered that she was an acquaintance and that I did not know what was wrong with her. I was told medical help would be provided only with her consent and she refused to give it. At that moment they all jumped on the truck and took off. I decided I was going to do the same. I had no feelings of guilt. I did more than anyone would be expected to do that night. She flatly refused medical care, so she was on her own.

"Andrea, I am tried and I am going home." I strongly suggested that she sleep in the car and attempt to drive home when she was feeling more clear-headed. I offered again a blanket and pillow, which she refused. I walked to my car, got in and never looked back.

It was 9:00 a.m. when I finally woke up that morning. I figured I had hit my pillow around 2:00. Well, I did get to bed early. Just early on the wrong day. My thoughts were racing and I found myself very anxious. I was worried. I decided to call Andrea. After a brief ring a young woman answered the phone.

"Is Andrea there?" I asked.

"She's sleeping. Who is this?"

"Linda Edmunds. Don't wake her, I just wanted to make sure she was ok?"

"Why wouldn't she be ok? Where did she go last night? What did she do?"

I could sense that the woman was getting very agitated. She started talking real fast and demanding answers. I was becoming uncomfortable. This must be Andrea's roommate. Andrea said she lived with a young woman and her small child. They had met at church and decided to share expenses. Andrea said her friend was a "nanny" and traveled often with the family she worked for. That was why her roommate did not know about the man who was abusing her in their apartment.

I told the roommate that I did not call to give out information, only to see if Andrea was all right. If she wanted to know about last night she would have to talk to Andrea.

That evening Tom and I were having some friends over for dinner. I shared the story of the night before. I was still unnerved by it all. My friend, being a fireman, shared with me the laws regarding medical assistance and consent. As long as Andrea proved she was of sound mind, which she did by answering the questions, medical care could not be forced on her. Jerry said it sounded as if she had a grand mal seizure, yet the duration of the episode seemed too long for a grand mal seizure. We threw around the idea that maybe the seizures were caused by AIDS. Possibly, the virus was invading the brain. Another possibility was drugs. Unfortunately, I never had a chance to look at her prescription pills to determine what she was taking medication for. It was all a mystery. All I knew for sure was, this was a troubled, sick young woman, who needed help.

As we were enjoying a cup of coffee after the meal, Andrea called. I immediately told her I could not talk to her, as I had company, but I was relieved that she was all right. She asked if I was mad at her and I reassured her I wasn't. I told her we would talk later.

The following morning I called Suzanne. I shared with her the events of the bizarre night with Andrea. I was just about to tell Suzanne that I hoped it was the last I saw of her friend. I would continue to pray for Andrea, but from afar. Suzanne interrupted my thoughts.

"Mom, I know that dealing with Andrea wasn't easy for you, but I want you to know that because you are who you are, and allow God to work through you, I am so proud that you are my mom. You always taught us to ask the question, *What would Jesus do?* Now you are showing us."

Urrrrrrr, I hated it when God spoke to me through my children.

andrea

About two months had gone by since I met Suzanne's mom at the hospital. I had called her a few times and we talked. She was always encouraging and I enjoyed talking to her. At this point in time, I did not have very many people who were thrilled with me. My parents were distressed over my inability to grow up. My sister was fed up with my lies and lack of self-control. My roommate was convinced that my odd behavior had to do with drinking or drugs, and since losing my job at UPS, I had no friends to speak of. I had lost contact with most of my high school friends, and had become too paranoid the last few years to attempt to make new friends.

On this particular morning in November I left my apartment early for another appointment downtown. I do not recall much of what happened that day except I somehow ended up at a market near the hospital. Confused and disoriented, I racked my brain to figure out where I was, and how I got there. Did I drive? If I did, where was my car? I checked my watch and saw it was 10:00 p.m. Where and what had I done that day? I tried to think, but it was as if something was blocking any thoughts from entering my head. I suspected I was in trouble and should call someone. Fortunately numbers come easily to me and that night was no exception. My problem was who to call. I was limited to who I could call to rescue me. I do recall hallucinating and feeling odd. These feelings were starting to become the norm. The AIDS virus was doing havoc on my brain.

I tried calling the Leonard's, but I couldn't get through... the line was busy. I called my friend Madeline, but she was all the way up in Seattle, Washington. So even though hearing a familiar voice was comforting, she was no help in getting me out of the predicament I was in. I tried to keep my problems to myself, so I didn't want to call my roommate. If she knew I got confused, I am sure she would not have wanted me to watch her child, which was the only reason I had a place to live. Calling my parents was absolutely out of the question. They had never seen me confused. My illness was not something I talked about. AIDS is not an easy thing to discuss with those you love.

It was cold out and I was nauseous. I had no idea if I had eaten that day. I had to pull myself together. Just then

On the Road to Peace

I remembered Linda. Of course I could call her. I tried her at work, but got the machine. Then I remembered how late it was. Of course she would not be at work. I called her at home. I knew that if I could somehow talk to her, she would make everything better.

Her husband Tom answered the phone, and when I asked to talk to Linda, he said she had already gone to bed. I told him that this was important and I really needed to talk to her. He suggested I talk to him. Frustrated, I did not want to explain to a stranger that I was confused and lost. I was about to hang up the phone when I heard Linda say hello.

The next thing I remember after talking to Linda on the phone is sitting in the driver's seat of my jeep. My watch said 4:30 a.m. The only thing I knew for sure was that I needed to get home. So I started up my car and headed home. I had driven the twenty plus miles up the freeway to my exit, and headed up the off ramp, when my jeep stalled at the stoplight. I tried restarting it, only to get it to sputter to life for a few short seconds and then stall again. Frustrated and extremely exhausted, I coasted it backward and off to the side of the road into the dirt.

After trying to get it to turn over a few times, I realized that I was once again having problems with this unreliable car of mine. So I engaged the parking brake and popped up the hood to see what the problem was. Like in my current state of mind, I could really figure it out.

Getting out of the car and raising the hood I was shocked to see a small electrical fire had started. With the rush of my adrenaline jolting me to my senses, I ripped my thick pullover jacket over my head and used it to try to snuff out the flames. Unfortunately, all I seemed to accomplish, was now not only was my Jeep on fire, but my flannel jacket was burning up as well.

Desperate to put out the fire, I ran back to the back seat, and got out my other jacket and put that one over the growing flames and then slammed down the hood thinking without so much oxygen the fire would go out.

Now with the hood closed, smoke was pouring out between the cracks and from below by the tires. Remembering something I heard about a lot of smoke meant the fire was out; I crouched down on my knees to look up underneath the engine.

I was horrified to see that the flames were growing and licking out everywhere. Just then a man who had pulled over to assist me came running across the street with a small fire extinguisher. But with the hood shut, he couldn't get to the flames. So I ran back to once again pop the hood. As soon as he touched the hot hood latch, his reflexes kicked in and he jerked his arms back. I expected him to try again, and when he didn't, I knew it was up to me to get this hood back open and somehow try to salvage my Jeep.

I didn't feel my fingers and hands burning as I fumbled for the latch to get it open. Finally I got it, and propped open the hood so the guy could spray the flames. He emptied out the whole canister without seeming to make a dent. He told me he had another one in his truck, and while he ran over to get it, I grabbed my burning jackets off the engine. I was thinking that they were the main source of the flames. I only succeeded in burning my hands even more and having the inner linings of the jackets melt to my fingers.

When the second extinguisher was empty, and the flames were getting more and more out of control, I realized it was a loss cause. My Jeep was going to burn.

I stood there for a few seconds just starring at the flames, when I thought, "Pickles!" I ran to the back door and grabbed my bear and blanket, my most prized possessions. Clutching them tightly, I backed away from the Jeep a few feet only to stare in despair at my new predicament. Then I instinctively felt my back pocket for my wallet. It wasn't there. And it had all the money I owned in it. Just over twenty dollars.

Franticly racking my brain I tried to remember what I had done with it when I'd gotten into my Jeep earlier that morning. I couldn't remember for sure, but I could bet I'd laid it on the front passenger seat with my small bag of meds.

Once again I ran back to my Jeep, only this time to the passenger side. Not being able to see between the darkness and the smoke, I felt around the seat with my hands. Not coming upon anything, I started feeling around on the floor.

All of a sudden I heard a loud "POP!" and the inside of my car suddenly lit up like someone had turned on a bright orange light. I glanced up and realized the sound I had heard was the windshield breaking and the light that was turned on was the dashboard on fire.

I had to make a tough decision, twenty dollars, or my life. My life won.

I backed out of the car and stepped away to watch my Jeep literally go up in flames. Soon after the fire department showed up and put out the fire in a few short minutes.

The stench was putrid and my Jeep was almost thoroughly gutted. Sadly I realized there was nothing left to salvage. But at least I still had my bear and blanket, and my life. Later one of the firemen came up to me and handed me my wallet, which somehow wasn't burned, but stinking and dripping wet. I was extremely grateful to him. Twenty bucks isn't much, but when it's all you got, it's a small fortune.

He then asked me if I was injured, motioning towards the burns on my hands. Looking down at them, for the first time they started to hurt. I told him I was fine, vaguely remembering telling another set of firemen earlier that night the same thing.

Since I only lived about a mile away, I told the firemen and the few cops that had gathered that I was going to walk home. But the cops told me I couldn't just leave my Jeep there on the side of the road.

Tired and burned and at the end of my rope, I forcefully told them that I'd be back later to deal with it. But they just as forcefully said that I would have to have it towed away immediately.

I was completely exhausted. My hands hurt from being burned. I was dizzy and my head was hurting from the noise going on in my brain. I was having trouble carrying on a conversation with the officer. At that moment I sadly regretted not being in the car when it burned.

Then one cop, being more intuitive than the others, came over to me and kindly asked me if there was someone he could call to come pick me up. Sighing I gave him my phone number so my roommate could come get me. After he called that in, he also called a tow truck for me and assured me that since my home was so close by, he would see to it that there would be no charge. He informed me that I'd have to make future arrangements to dispose of it legally. I made a mental note to thank God later for this angel among my crisis.

When I got home shortly later, I layed down and fell asleep as soon as my head hit the pillow. I was exhausted. I'd had a hard night, even for me.

It seemed as if I had just closed my eyes when my roommate came charging into my room yelling for me to wake up. Now what, I thought.

"You weren't at the Leonard's last night. You were with Linda, you liar!"

Blinking my eyes and a little disoriented, I tried to focus on her. I didn't recall telling her I was going to the Leonard's, or did I. Often I would go up to their place for the weekend. I guess if I was not home for the night that would be her assumption.

'You and Linda were out all night long!"

"I was not!" I shouted back at her, thinking she was talking about Linda Leonard, who at the time was living in New York City. I was tired and a little disoriented, but not to the point I would not have remembered flying to New York and back.

"You are such a liar! I just got off the phone with her. She called to see if you were okay," she said, emphasizing the *okay* very sarcastically.

"Why wouldn't you be okay Andrea? What did you do last night that would make her question if you were okay?"

"Nothing" I mumbled back, just wanting to go back to sleep.

As I tried to go back to sleep, my mind started wandering. Vaguely I started to remember that I was with Linda last night, but not Linda Leonard, but Linda, Suzanne's mom. I recalled her soothing voice asking me if I wanted a ride home. Then suddenly I visualized my jeep on fire.

Oh no, I thought to myself. What had I done last night? What had I told Linda? Had I hurt her? The questions were swirling in my mind. I suddenly felt an intense headache coming on and feared a seizure. I recalled nothing whatsoever in between calling Linda and my jeep being on fire. Except for haunting bits and pieces, that to this day makes no sense to me.

Laying my head back down on the pillow and staring at the ceiling, I wondered why so much drama had to happen to me. Other people didn't live like this, did they? Losing time? Getting confused? Hearing Voices? Seeing demons? As I laid there totally overwhelmed with my life, little did I know that in exactly one week I would be moving all my stuff out of my apartment, to embark on a new life. I was to embark on a new life under the guidance of a woman whom I would come to know as "Boss."

Do not merely listen to the word, and so deceive yourselves. Do what it says. James 1:22

Chapter Three

The Invitation

linda

Suzanne called me one evening and said she heard that on Thanksgiving Eve our church was hosting a husband and wife team called "The Potter's Wheel." The husband molds clay on stage while his wife sings. Suzanne had seen them once before and was excited that they were coming to our church.

"Mom, would you take Andrea to church that night, I can't come down or else I would take her myself. I know she would like it. She's into art and music."

Not wanting to turn down my daughter's desire to reach out, I said ok. "I'll call Andrea tomorrow and ask her."

I did have an interest in seeing the performance myself, and knew that Tom would be studying.

I called Andrea the next day and invited her. She was delighted. She said it had been along time since she had been to church. Her comment made me curious as to where her heart was in relationship to God.

The day of the performance she called me twice to ask what time I was going to pick her up and for reassurance that I wasn't going to "flake" on her. I remember thinking that she must have been let down often in her life by others.

I rushed home from work, showered and changed. I had promised I would pick up Andrea at 5:30 p.m. I felt it would be a bad idea to be late.

I was proud of myself for finding, not only the complex, but also her apartment. This was the third time I had visited her place, but this time I was more relaxed. The first time, even though I planned just to leave the Bible at the door, I was anxious. The thought of seeing someone the age of my children, dying of such a horrendous disease, was disturbing. The second time, just last week, I was so stressed out because of Andrea's behavior, I would not have remembered my own apartment number, much less hers.

I knocked. I knocked again. After all this, could she not be home? As I started to walk away I heard the door open. Andrea looked at me as if she was deciding whether or not she wanted to go.

The door closed and I found myself standing out in front of her apartment for the next five minutes. Finally the door opened again and she walked out very reluctantly. She walked behind me. Every time I turned around to see if she was following me, she would stop and step back. She wouldn't move again until I started walking.

As we walked, a Persian cat walked passed me. I turned to look at the cat as Andrea was bent down to pick it up. She carried the cat to my car.

"Is that *your* cat?"

"Yeah," she replied holding the cat closer to her chest.

"What's her name?"

"Sophia."

"She's pretty." I put my hand on the handle of my car door. Sensing that Andrea wanted to bring the cat with her.

"Andrea, you need to put Sophia down now, we must get going or we will be late."

With a childlike expression Andrea asked, "Can't we bring her with us?"

"Of course not. Last time I took notice, cats did not attend church."

Reluctantly she put the cat down and stood looking at me.
"Are you going to get in?"
Slowly she got in.
"What's the matter Andrea, don't you want to go to church? It'll be fun."

To this day many adjectives have been used to describe that night with Andrea at church, but "fun" has never been one of them. Little did I know what was in store for the two of us.

The minute Andrea was seated in the car she rolled down the window. The cold air during the drive was very uncomfortable to me, but I did not want to rock the boat. If this is what she needed to do, so be it. She told me many months later that she felt claustrophobic in my small car and having the window down helped. I learned early in our relationship that her odd behavior always had a logical explanation. She also told me that the reason she always wore a baseball cap was to keep all the stuff in her head from falling out. Gee...makes sense to me.

I was satisfied that we had arrived early enough to get a good seat in the front. As we sat down I could see that Andrea was anxious. The more anxious she seemed, the more anxious I became. It seemed like hours before the program began. Finally the "Potter" started. It was loud for my ears so I knew it had to be loud for Andrea. I noticed that she had both her hands in a fist and was rubbing her head. I recalled her doing this a lot the night at Ralph's Market when she was having so many problems.

Andrea leaned slightly towards me and mumbled, "I need to go to the car and get my medicine."

"I'll go with you," I replied.

"What's the matter, don't you trust me?" she said looking hurt.

Since trust was a big issue with her, I let her go alone. Besides I thought it would draw too much attention if both of us walked out. I prayed that I was making the right decision. She did come back, but stayed only ten minutes before announcing she needed to go to the bathroom. I then wished

I hadn't decided to sit so close to the front. I turned around for a brief moment as she walked down the isle. She was staggering. I assumed her illness had affected her gait. Maybe Andrea's theory of the AIDS virus penetrating her brain was correct.

I could not relax. Andrea had not returned. I realized at that moment that Andrea had not given me back my car keys from the first trip out to the car. I started to panic. It could not take that long to go to the bathroom. I knew I had to go check on her.

My intuition told me something was wrong and I needed to leave. I grabbed my Bible, purse, and jacket. Even if Andrea was ok, I was not going to walk back up to the front. We would have to watch the program from the back.

I went into the bathroom and called her name. I didn't see anyone. I ran out to the car. Thank goodness my car was still there. As I peeked in, I could see that her teddy bear and blanket, which she reluctantly left in the front seat, was still there. That was a good sign. I didn't think she would go far without them.

I found myself running all around the church grounds. Where could she have gone? I felt sick to my stomach. Something was wrong! I went back into the church and looked down towards the front to see if she had returned. No, she hadn't. I decided to go back and check the bathroom again. Again I called her name. Nothing. Just as I was turning around I had a thought. I got down on my knees and looked under the stalls. Sure enough, I spotted a pair of very large black tennis shoes in the stall farthest from me. They were Andrea's.

"Andrea! Andrea, are you all right? Andrea! Andrea, answer me!"

"Uh, who are you? I don't recognize your voice, I don't know who you are," came a soft timid voice from behind the stall door.

"Yes, you do, I'm Linda, Suzanne's mom, I brought you to church."

Still sounding frightened, she repeated, "I don't think I know you."

"Yes, you do, come on out and look at me," I said, exasperated.

After a few minutes, I finally convinced her to come out of the stall. She staggered out. She didn't look right. Something was terribly wrong. Why was she looking at me so oddly? I didn't have time to think, I needed to get her home.

I was having flashbacks of the previous weekend. I had to get her out of the church.

Without warning, just as we were approaching the large doors to the outside, her body started swaying and she slowly crumbled to the ground. Within seconds two men who were standing close by, came to her rescue. Andrea went wild. She started swearing at them to get away from her. Her language made me cringe.

I was mortified. She was swearing at the top of her lungs in my church. Quickly I looked to see if the doors to the sanctuary were shut. Thank goodness, the doors had been closed.

I pleaded, "Please step back, she is afraid of you. Come on Andrea, let me help you up and we will walk out together."

As the men backed away she ran out the front door. I was running behind her and the two men were running behind me. As I caught up with her, she backed herself up against a wall of the church. Her eyes told me she was scared. As Ray, the Associate Pastor, approached her, she became verbally abusive towards him.

As he got close he smelled liquor on her breath. "You're drunk, you've been drinking," exclaimed Ray.

"I am not drunk," she shouted back, "I have AIDS, and I suffer from dementia. I get confused, that's all. I am not drunk!"

Ray looked at me and said, "She has liquor on her breath."

In a defiant voice Andrea screamed, "What are you going to do, call the cops?"

"I am a cop," said Ray with a firm voice.

I couldn't believe she was drunk. I had been with her now for the last two hours. When would she have had time to drink enough to make her drunk? Would not I have smelled it on her breath when she got in the car? It just didn't make sense.

The men insisted she had been drinking. I was embarrassed. I brought someone to church drunk. Why couldn't I smell it? As the three of us stood back, Andrea was stumbling and falling on the ground, without attempting to break her fall. She was hitting her head with such force I thought for sure she was going to split her head wide open. Every time one of us made a motion towards her, she would jump up and step back, not taking her eyes off of us. One of the men, Jim, started talking to her in a calming voice. She seemed to be more receptive to him. He told her that no one was going to hurt her that we only wanted to help. He was suggesting we move away from the entrance of the church towards the parking lot. I thought, good idea. I would have preferred a big hole open up and she drop into it and disappear, but moving her and her antics to the parking lot was my second choice.

I was hoping I could get her into the car and leave. I wanted to be as far away from my church as soon as possible. As we got to the parking lot, I pointed to where my car was and said I would take it from there. Both men looked at me like I was crazy. They had no intentions of leaving her alone with me.

As all of us were walking into the parking lot, Andrea fell to the ground, flat on her back. Jim was trying to hold her down when she started having a seizure. Another Associate Pastor joined us, got on his knees and started praying for her. I heard someone say that the paramedics were on their way.

The fire station is across the street from our church and in a matter of minutes an ambulance was approaching us. I don't recall the paramedics asking any questions or giving Andrea the option of refusing medical care. She was acting out of her mind and there were so many witnesses. As soon as Andrea saw the ambulance she went ballistic. By this time she had three men restraining her.

As I watched the commotion, I noticed people walking towards the parking lot. I looked at my watch and in horror realized church was over. I panicked. Before I could complete the thought in my head, *"I hope these people don't find out that I am the one who brought this woman to church,"* Andrea yelled out, as they were putting her on the stretcher:

"I want Linda...I want Linda, where is my friend Linda!"

(Isn't it just like God to humble us when we need it?)

Just prior to closing the doors to the ambulance, Andrea asked for her stuff. She wanted her backpack, blanket and teddy bear. I ran to my car and grabbed her things off the front seat of the car. I asked the paramedics where they were going to take her and they wouldn't tell me. Everyone told me to go home. I jumped in my car thinking I would follow the ambulance, but because everyone was trying to get out of the parking lot at the same time, I got caught behind some cars, and the ambulance took off without me.

Tom greeted me at the front door. One thing I could always count on was a warm smile and a hug from him. His greeting was not only welcomed but also needed.

"How did it go, Hon?"

"Beyond anything anyone could have ever imagined."

As we sat on the couch, I started sharing what had happened that night. Tom, seeing that I was discouraged and frustrated, encouraged me to pray for Andrea and to keep in mind that God had a plan. I, too, believed God had a plan for Andrea; I just didn't want it to include me.

Tom and I went to bed. Tom fell asleep immediately, however sleep did not come that easily for me.

Before I realized that the phone was ringing, the answering machine came on. I glanced at the clock on the bed stand. Who would be calling at 1:20 in the morning? I listened as the caller started to speak. It was Andrea.

"Hey, Linda...they want to take me to jail. Hey, you have to come get me."

By this time, Tom was stirring in bed. "Who is it, Hon?"

"It's Andrea, she wants me to come get her."

I could hear the machine disconnect. She didn't say where she was, which was a relief to me. Couldn't rescue her if I didn't know where she was.

Just then, the phone rang again. Again, I let the machine get the call. "Hey Linda, they want to send me to jail, I need you to come get me. Why did you have them take me away? Please, pick up the phone."

My heart was breaking. I wanted to go get her, yet something inside me was telling me that I shouldn't. Please God make it clear, what I should do? The phone rang again, but the caller hung up without leaving a message. Needless to say my mind was racing with thoughts and I did not sleep at all that night.

The next day was Thanksgiving. Tom and I had plans to celebrate at the home of our best friends. I was working in the kitchen when the phone rang. It was Andrea.

"Hey Linda, why didn't you pick up the phone last night?"

"Andrea, correction, early this morning...very early. Where are you now?"

"Doesn't matter."

Curious, I asked, "Who came to get you?"

Andrea said that since she could not get anyone to come get her, the hospital called the police to take her home. She said that her roommate got very angry with her after she got home and kicked her out.

"Where are you now, Andrea?" I asked.

"I'm at the Leonards."

"Are these the parents of your high school friend?"

"Yes, but I can't stay here. They don't know I am here."

"How did you get in?" I asked, wondering if I really wanted to know.

"I know which doors they tend to leave unlocked. I just wanted to use the phone. Linda, I don't want to live. I have no job, my roommate kicked me out, and I have nowhere to go. I am going to end it today. Life is too hard."

"Andrea, what do you plan on doing?"

"It shouldn't matter to you, but will you do me a favor?"

"What?" I asked hesitantly, without making a commitment.

"Will you tell the Leonards that I have appreciated all that they have done for me through the years, and that they were the only real friends I've ever had. Tell them that I love them."

I saw an opportunity. Andrea had been very evasive in giving me information about her parents, her sister, her roommate, or anyone else in her life. It was as if she was afraid I would try and make contact, and for some reason she did not want that to happen.

"Yes Andrea, of course I'll give them the message, give me their phone number."

She gave it to me. Now I had the name and number of people who knew her. She needed a family member or a friend to get involved. I was hoping I had seen the last of Andrea Nelson. However, my gut instincts told me I would see her again, and I was right.

andrea

I was excited about going to church. It had been almost six years since I attended any church. During my first year of college, I got involved in a church, which proved to be what most Bible believers would call a religious cult. Even though the experience made me bitter towards organized religion, deep down inside I felt the void. I still desired to be close to God.

Looking back on the experience I can see how easy it was for me to get involved with the group. Being insecure, I was easy prey. My paranoia fed right into it too. I was constantly afraid of 'demonic people' who were out to get me. What better place to be than to be surrounded by Godly people.

Involved heavily sounds like an understatement though. After my baptism into the church, I was forced to leave my parents' house and move in with one of the "sisters" in the congregation. If you were single you *had* to live with another family from the church. There were no exceptions. Accountability was a big issue. I was accountable to my new church family.

Everything you did, every decision you made had to go through the Advisors. We were all considered "disciples." Not Christians, because that was too general. Each disciple had a "discipleler". This discipleler would tell you everything from how you should interact with your spouse to what car you should buy.

Only those in their church were going to heaven, for they were the *only true* body of Christ. Anyone who left the church was considered to have "fallen away." No one was to have relations with them in any way. They, who fell, were to be avoided at all times.

On my initial joining of the church, everything was warm and fuzzy. People were calling me, inviting me to all sorts of events. There was Bible studies, mid-week night services, and Sunday services in downtown San Diego, at the Convention Center. Hundreds would attend. I wasn't a big fan of being surrounded by so many people, but I felt like I had so many new friends, it didn't really matter. There were also fun events like parties and movie outings. There were softball, volleyball, and soccer games. They had picnics all of which I was invited. Warm people that seemed to like me and really care about me were always surrounding me. Acceptance by others was never easy, so I felt very special with my new family.

Once you were baptized into the church, you were thrown a party, and accepted even more. Then they had you move in with them, and soon you were inviting others, encouraging them to come to these events and be baptized.

They had me move in with a woman named June. She was divorced, and had two kids. June had a girl six years old and a boy who was eight. I became close to them, and we became like a family. She got me a job baby-sitting for a woman she knew, and everything seemed perfect. I lived with them for nine months, until I was finally disfellowshiped. I'm assuming because of my bizarre behavior, and not being very compliant. Or it possibly could have been that it was leaked out that I had AIDS. In either case, it was never made clear to me.

Now eight years later, once again I was being invited to church. For whatever reason, when Linda invited me I wanted to go. Maybe it was my eagerness to see her again, or maybe it was because I knew Suzanne really wanted me to go. For whatever reason, I accepted.

Excited about it, and knowing that my mom had been pressuring me for the last year to get involved in a church, I called to tell her I was going to church. I explained that Linda was the mom of a friend.

Unfortunately or fortunately, I remember very little about that night at church. I do remember Linda picking me up and taking me to church. I recall seeing more people than I had expected. Linda took me all the way up to the second row of the sanctuary. I would have preferred to sit way in the back, isolated. But being in the front on the right side of the curve of seats, I could see all the people along my left looking my way from their side of the curve, and they were all pointing at me and talking about me, hundreds of them. They were all yelling that I was possessed and a liar and a whore and drunk, and that there was no place for me in their church.

That was enough for me. I had to get out of there. I had a beer and some zannex in the car, in my backpack. I was sure I was entitled to something to calm me down, cause I was on the verge of a seizure.

The next thing I remember was I was in a hospital with my arms and feet restrained to the bed, and all I had on was my underwear and a hospital gown. I recalled absolutely nothing after I left Linda sitting in the second row of her church.

There was a male security officer standing in my doorway facing the other way as if he was guarding my room. I was curious about him but first I had to get out of these restraints. I don't know how I did it, but I got free and lowered the side of my bed so I could get up and get dressed. I wasn't about to spend any more time here in this hospital.

Hearing the noise of my bed rail going down, the guard turned around, and looked at me astonished that I was free and standing. He hesitated for a second as if contemplating what to do, and then started to come towards me.

That's when I ripped off my robe and stood there half naked and started swearing at him that I'd sue both him and the hospital for sexual harassment if he tried to touch me.

From my past experiences with the police, I'd learned something from my term of probation... that only a female officer could search me, and so I thought I had some sort of case if this man tried to touch me while I was half naked.

It worked and he immediately backed off and turned around and started hollering for a nurse. But by the time anybody came, I was fully dressed and had my bear and blanket and I was ready to walk out the door. The only problem was I was at least thirty-five miles from home with no way to get there.

The nurses made it obvious they did not want me to just waltz out the door with no plan for transportation. They suspected that if I left and started wandering the streets, I would undoubtedly be back that night. So they gave me a phone.

Calling for a ride, I started out with the one I felt was most responsible for me. The one who had gotten me into this predicament. The one who had taken me to church, Linda.

Upon getting her answering machine a couple times instead of her, I realized I wasn't getting anywhere, so I decided to try my old faithful friends in times like these; the Leonard's. I was relieved that Pamela answered the phone. I thought I had a better chance with her than Arnold, but after I told her where I was, she firmly responded that a night in the hospital would be good for me. She offered to pick me up in the morning.

The nurses on staff and I both agreed on one thing. We both wanted me out of there. So I called Suzanne. But when I realized that Suzanne couldn't help me, I started getting extremely frustrated. Not only was I frustrated, but also I could sense the building of frustration with the nurses.

The staff decided to call me a taxi. But I told them I didn't have any money for a cab. They must have really wanted me out of there because they were willing to pay for it. But then when the cab driver showed up, I got paranoid and was too afraid to get in the car. Then they called the cops and requested they take me home. I was afraid of the cops, but at least there were two of them, and I'd really wanted to get home, and I figured that at least they were accountable to each other. So I got into the police car.

When they got to my apartment complex, they asked me if this is where I lived. Recognizing it, I said yes. They dropped me there on the outskirts and left.

A little confused, it took me about a half-hour to find my apartment. Once I found it I reached in my pocket and realized I did not have my keys. I must have lost them sometime during the evening. I would need to climb in my bedroom window.

With my body halfway in my room, my roommate came in, turned on the light, and immediately started yelling at me. She wanted to know where I had been all night and why was I crawling into my bedroom window.

I begged her to leave me alone because I'd just gotten out of the hospital, but she didn't believe me. Thinking I was drunk, she called me a few choice words like, "Drunk", "Drug addict", and "Liar".

Completely at her wits end with my bizarre behavior, she kicked me out. She and her daughter were leaving for Palm Springs in the morning for a few days, and she wanted me out when they returned. She had temporarily kicked me out before, and then taken me back, but I knew this was it. She meant what she said. She wanted me gone. I didn't even try to stay in the apartment. With everything that happened the last ten hours, I wasn't going to deal with her anger.

When I woke up in the early morning light, I wondered what I was doing in my roommate's car. After a few minutes of thinking about it, I remembered what had happened last night. It seemed like at least a week since I had gone to church with Linda, yet it was only twelve hours ago.

Thoughts flooded my head. I hated how I felt all the time. I hated getting confused and disoriented. I hated being alone, and not having friends. I hated not having any control over my life. I hated how others viewed me. I hated who I had become.

Trust in the Lord with all your heart, and lean not on your own understanding; in all your way acknowledge Him, and He will direct your path. Proverb 3:5-6

Chapter Four

The Commitment

linda

I realized that I needed to talk to Suzanne. I was sure she was anxious to hear how Andrea liked our church. Boy, talk about a story. After going over all the bizarre events of the evening, Suzanne was at a loss for words.

"Mom, I am so sorry it did not work out. What is wrong with her? Is it the AIDS that is causing her to act this way?"

"I don't know sugar, but something is very wrong. I don't know enough about AIDS to make an intelligent assessment. I certainly can understand why she is depressed. She doesn't seem to have much going for her."

I asked Suzanne if she ever heard Andrea mention the Leonards. Suzanne hadn't. I told Suzanne that Andrea was talking about taking her life. She had given me the telephone number of the Lenoards and had asked me to give them a message in case of suicide.

We spent Thanksgiving Day with our dear friends. Our kids are close, so it makes getting together fun for all. The episode of the previous night was fresh on my mind as I went to bed that night. I had tried often calling the number Andrea gave me, but got no answer.

Tom and I pray together before going to bed. His prayers always comfort me, but that night they were especially touching. Having never met Andrea, he prayed for her as if she was someone he knew very well, who was close to his heart.

I found myself jumping out of bed startled as the phone was ringing. Good grief, what time was it? I tried to focus on the wall clock as I ran to the kitchen to pick up the phone. It was 4:00 am.

"Hello, Mom, Andrea is up here."

"What?"

"She showed up around midnight. I think she was drunk, she was acting weird, and she looked a mess. She said something about having a shotgun and robbing a bank."

"Where is she now?"

"I don't know, the last time I saw her she was passed out by her car. I can see from my window her car in the parking lot, so I know she is still here."

"Did you see the gun?"

"No."

"Honey, I will get dressed now. Do not go looking for her, do not answer your phone, and do not let her into your dorm."

"Mom, I didn't stay in my room last night because I was scared, I stayed with friends. Here is the number where you can reach me when you arrive."

As Tom was making me coffee to go, I was throwing on my clothes. Then I decided it was time to give Andrea's friends a call. I didn't care how early it was.

As a sleepy voice answered in a weak "hello," I started talking fast. "I don't have much time. Andrea is up in San Luis Obispo with my daughter. She says she doesn't want to live and is planning on ending her life. She says she has a gun. I am on my way up there, but before I leave, I want you to tell me what I need to know about this kid. What is wrong with her?"

By this time, the woman's voice had changed and I knew she was now wide-awake. "Well, she has AIDS and it affects the way she thinks. She has seizures often and we assume it is because of the AIDS. She has done some drugs, but has been clean for about five years. I can't imagine where she would get a gun. We have seen her get quite wild, but she has never hurt anyone. She has a lot of problems, but has never given us the impression that she would consider taking her life."

The woman at that point obviously turned to her husband, who also had been awakened by my call. "Arnold, do you think that about covers it?" I heard a male's voice say "yes."

Coffee in one hand, keys in the other and a backpack over my shoulder, I was out the door. The drive under normal conditions took me exactly five hours. This morning I made it in record time...four hours and ten minutes. I was a mom on a mission.

As I drove into the deserted college campus I wasn't quite sure what I was going to do. The first thing I needed was a bathroom. I needed to be relieved of the coffee I had drunk on the way up.

The college dorms had an interesting layout. Branching out from a large recreation room were two doors leading to eight towers. You had to go into the recreation room, go through one of the doors on opposite ends of the room, in order to get to the towers. Suzanne lived in one of the towers.

As I ran into the recreation room, all I could think about was finding the nearest bathroom. After that I would find a phone and call the number Suzanne gave me.

I entered what seemed at first like a deserted room. Then I heard music in the background. At first I wasn't sure where it was coming from. As pleasant as the sound was to my rattled nerves, I did not have time to enjoy it; I needed to find a bathroom.

I ran in and out of corridors.

As I came around a corner, I found myself face to face with Andrea.

"Are you running from me?" she asked.

"No, I have been in the car the last four and a half hours and I was looking for a bathroom."

"Over there," she pointed

"Don't move, Andrea, I'll be right back."

At least she wasn't with Suzanne. Everything seemed pretty calm, considering.

I went to the bathroom quickly. Andrea obviously wasn't into obedience, because when I returned, she was gone.

Then again I heard the music and singing in the background.

I looked towards the music, this time trying to focus. Oh my gosh....It was Andrea at the piano!

The closer I got to her, the more amazed I was. As I stood looking down at her play and sing, I could hardly believe my eyes and ears. Her hair looked as if it hadn't been washed or combed in days. She had on the same clothes the night she was taken away in the ambulance at my church, only now they had oil and dirt all over them. She was sporting a black eye, and the whole side of her face was scraped.

Andrea kept on playing and singing as she looked up at me and smiled. Even in her disarray, there was innocent sweetness about her.

I called Suzanne and she said she would come down. After we embraced and I could see she was all right, I turned to Andrea and demanded she sit down with Suzanne and me. We needed to have a serious talk.

"What happened to your face Andrea?"

"Nothing," she said as she took her hand and brushed her hair back behind her ear.

"Don't tell me nothing, you have a black eye and the whole right side of your face is scrapped and crusted with blood."

Andrea just looked at me and smiled as if to say, I am sure glad to see you.

I asked again, "Are you going to tell me what happened?"

"You do not want to know."

"Yes, I do want to know." I repeated with irritation.

Sheepishly she mumbled, "I think I killed someone."

"Who?"

"Craig."

"How?"

"I went to his house and did something awful."

"What?" I was almost afraid to ask.

"I injected him with poison," she responded with a guilty smile.

"Is this for real?"

Andrea nodded.

"Andrea, are you telling me the truth? Where was his family?"

"They weren't home. I think he is dead. I really don't know. What should I do? I also have a shotgun."

"Where is the gun?" I asked, looking around nervously.

"I can't tell you," she said, glancing quickly at Suzanne.

"What were you planning on doing with the gun?" I asked rather sarcastically.

"I was going to rob a bank and have the police shoot me,." she replied.

"And what made you change your mind?"

"The banks were closed."

"Of course Andrea, this is Thanksgiving weekend."

(I read much later, ten percent of police shootings between 1996 and 1997 fit the pattern of "shooting-by-cop" phenomenon. It's a form of suicide).

Suzanne and I looked at each other suspiciously. The story was too farfetched to be creditable. Besides, Andrea was not acting like someone who had just killed someone. And for someone who wanted to end her life yesterday, she seemed to be in a pretty good mood now. I was fairly convinced that she was telling a wild fable.

"Hey, you guys, I am so glad you are here," Andrea said with a twinkle in her eyes that couldn't go unnoticed.

"Andrea, this is serious!"

"But I have a plan," she said with a giggle.

"Well, Andrea, so do I, and we are going to discuss my plan. Since you are determined to be in our lives, we are going to set some boundaries."

The first order of business was the gun. I asked Andrea if she was telling the truth about a gun. She replied very sheepishly, yes. She would not give me any more information as to where the gun was or where she got it. Of course, I was very suspicious so I did not push the issue.

"Andrea, here is the plan. I have six things I would like you to do."

"First, I want you to return the gun to its rightful owner. Second, you must move out of your apartment. Third, I want you to call your social worker and request she call me. Fourth, make an appointment to see your doctor. Fifth, read your Bible at least ten minutes every day. Sixth, thank God for two things each evening before you go to bed."

The only demand I figured would be difficult was the second one. Andrea had lived with Doris, her friend for six years. Andrea said that although Doris kicked her out, Doris would change her mind. Doris needed Andrea. Ever since Andrea was fired from UPS, nine months earlier, Andrea's days consisted of taking care of the needs of Doris's seven-year-old daughter. Apparently, now that Andrea did not have a job, she would take care of the child in exchange for her room and board. It was a win-win situation.

When I questioned how Doris could possibly not know of the rape and abuse going on in her apartment, Andrea explained that he would never come around when Doris or the young girl were home. If Doris knew of Craig she would kick Andrea out for good. Andrea said she could not take that chance. The story did not seem logical, but I was not going to take any chances. I had to find a safe place for Andrea to live.

I asked Andrea if she had anyone she could stay with for a few days. I did not want her going back to her apartment and I needed time to make other arrangements. She said she could probably go stay with the Leonards. Before I knew it, I was on the phone for the second time that morning bothering those kind people.

"Good morning again, this is Linda Edmunds. I am now up in San Luis Obispo with Andrea. Would it be possible for her to come stay with you a few days until I can find her a safe place to stay?"

Without hesitation, they said yes. Andrea said they knew all about Craig and were probably thrilled that she had decided to do something about it. Apparently, they were the "friends" who had suggested she write a book. They were the ones, besides Madeline, in whom she always confided.

Once I felt confident that Andrea understood what she needed to do, I insisted that she get back in her car and head toward San Diego.

Andrea did not seem anxious to get back on the road, but I insisted. Suzanne and I had looked forward to this time together and I wanted to enjoy it without any distractions. I reminded Andrea that her first promise was to return the gun. I asked her if it was loaded and she said no. She did say she had bullets, and I insisted that she give them to me. She said she didn't want to, but she promised to throw them away. At this point, I was thinking that this gun story was just a bluff. At least I was praying so.

As Andrea stood by her car and we were exchanging last minute instructions, I asked her to give me a hug. She immediately took a few steps back and said,

"I don't do hugs."

As she drove away, Suzanne looked at me and said, "I give it two months."

"You don't think she will stick to her part of the deal?" I asked, having my own reservations.

"No mom, I was talking about the hug. I will give it two months before you will have her hugging you." Just then I gave Suzanne a hug. She was a terrific kid.

andrea

Contemplating my life and the severity of my problems, I mentally scanned my options. I realized I really didn't have any. I'd lost my job, then my car, and now a place to live. I had no money. The only friends I had were the Leonard's, and I was obviously wearing them down. I was scared of Craig and his abuse. I was infected with a fatal infectious disease, and on top of all that, I heard Voices and saw demons. I was losing my mind. I couldn't think of one thing that I had going for me.

I toyed with the idea of calling my sister and asking if I could stay with her for a while, but disregarded that option quickly. We had drifted apart during the years. It would be too uncomfortable. The thought of calling my parents for help made me anxious. I justified my anxiety due to their house being full of antiques. If I had a spell or seizure of some sorts I was bound to break something. The truth of the matter was; I did not want my parents to see how pitiful I had become.

There was nothing left to fight for, except my dignity, and I was going to salvage it once and for all.

Feeling good about my plans, I waited until my roommate left and then went inside to get a few things. Then I went back out to her car and started heading up to the Leonard's. But this time I wasn't heading up to their home to talk to them or to get patched up, or even for a place to crash... no, this time I was going there to get something else. I was going there to get a gun. I knew exactly where Arnold's guns were kept.

When I got to the Leonard's, they were home, but I could tell they were getting ready to leave. They were heading up to Pamela's mother's home for Thanksgiving. I could smell the turkey that had just come out of the oven. I could see two perfectly shaped pies on the counter. I had a twinge of jealously that they were so normal, heading out for the holiday to meet with family for a dinner feast. I thought of my own family getting together, but I couldn't remember if we were or not. I knew we always did, but I was a little confused, and wasn't sure if I was invited. But I knew that even if I was expected there, it would not be in the condition I was in. Besides, today I was busy. I had something to accomplish that in my mind was long overdue.

Leaving the Leonard's to allow them to get ready; I went for a drive with intentions to come back in an hour. They'd be gone, and I could get the gun, and carry on with my plan.

After driving around for a while, I headed back to the Leonard's. I went around the side of the house. Sure enough the sliding glass door into their dinning room was unlocked. Once inside the house and with the gun in my hand, I sat down at the kitchen counter. I felt comfortable in their place, even to the point of feeling at home. Feeling a little sentimental, I felt like saying goodbye to a few people. So first I called Madeline, and left her a message of thanks for the many nights of listening to me. Then I called Linda because in my mind we had some un-finished business. I was still hurt that she didn't answer the phone when I called her from the hospital.

I was glad that Linda was still home. I knew she had some big plans to join friends for Thanksgiving later that day. I wanted the Leonard's to know how thankful I was for all they'd done, and asked Linda if she could relay that message to them. Linda agreed and asked for their phone number. Linda definitely had a calming effect on me. It was something about her voice. Pushing it out of my head, I focused on my execution. The Voices were cheering me on and with the huge cloud of depression over me, I was glad everything was about to come to an end. It was obvious to me that the AIDS was taking too long, and something had to be done.

Then finally I called Suzanne. That conversation was a little more difficult. She was upset and even crying at some points. She seemed to sense that I was suicidal, even though I hadn't told her. I knew she was hurting for me, so I ended the conversation and hung up.

Excited that by the time the sun went down, I'd be peacefully dead, I headed back to San Diego. I planned to pick out a good Bank. While driving I went through a mental list of provisions the establishment would have to have. It would have to have large windows and a lot of open space inside so I could keep all the hostages away from me and be an easy target to the snipers. Some tall buildings with good spaces to hide and get aim from would be good too. I didn't want this to take any longer than possible. I had to pull it off right. I wasn't about to go back to jail. I would have to be killed.

Driving around town after town for hours, I just couldn't find a bank that was open. I didn't connect the fact that it was

On the Road to Peace

Thanksgiving Day, and banks weren't open. I wasn't thinking that clearly. I entertained the thought of a grocery store, but the Voices told me that it had to be a bank. As it approached early evening, I decided to put off my plan until tomorrow. I didn't think it would work in the dark. Besides, my hostages would need to get home to have dinner or be with their families and get some sleep. I didn't want to interfere with their lives too much. Once again, irrational thinking on my part.

I decided I had to do something to kill time. I was too scared to go home, and not wanting to go to the Leonard's for fear they might read my mind, I decided to drive up to San Luis Obispo where Suzanne was going to college. It had been bothering me all day that I had upset her. I didn't want to leave on a bad note with her.

I left around 5pm and got up there after midnight. All I had was Suzanne's address, but I was confident I could find her. Once on campus I realized that it wasn't going to be that easy. The college was huge. In desperation I knocked on a door and a young male student answered. Once again, irrational thinking; who goes to a strangers door after midnight to ask directions? Lucky for me, he was still awake and a nice guy. I showed him the address and asked him if he knew where it was. He told me that it was in a dormitory up on the far side of campus. It did not take me long after that to find the dormitory. I parked in a large parking lot across the street.

As I came up to the large building, I discovered I couldn't just waltz in. All the doors were locked. I wandered around for a while. I saw a group of kids walking up to the door. One of them pulled out a key and opened the door. I walked up behind them and slipped in before the door shut. I looked around for a while without much luck. This was a lot more difficult that I expected. Now that I was in, I still didn't know how to go about finding Suzanne. All the towers looked alike. I could feel my head getting fuzzy. Then I heard some talking and saw a group coming out of a hallway. I walked up to them and asked if any of them knew Suzanne. I hadn't even said her last name when they immediately told me with a smile where to find her.

I wasn't surprised that she was obviously popular and well liked. I myself liked her a lot. She really was a good person.

As I headed to the tower where I had been directed, I was very pleased with myself. After driving seven hours and then locating her, it was equivalent to finding a needle in a haystack. But as soon as Suzanne opened her door and saw me I could tell by the look on her face that she was not nearly as happy to see me, as I was to see her. In fact she looked terrified. I didn't really know what to say or do, but she sure did. Immediately she asked me how I got there and when I said I drove, she asked me where I had parked my car. She then started escorting me back to my car. I was a little hurt, but also impressed. Suzanne was very confident about what she was going to deal with in life, and it was obviously not going to be me that evening. Here she was twenty years old, and more mature than most of my friends who were much older.

I remember walking with her, then feeling very dizzy, and falling to the ground. Suzanne tried to pick me up. I told her that I couldn't get up.

"Andrea, then pray."

"Ok," I said a little uncomfortably.

"Andrea, I can't hear you."

"I am praying!"

"I want you to talk to God and I want to hear you."

I am assuming that I either satisfied Suzanne or made her mad, because the next time I opened my eyes I was laying on a sidewalk all by myself. I realized I was next to my car. I got up and laid down in the back seat. I had a splitting headache.

Once again I woke up to the sun while sleeping in the back seat of the car. I wondered what I had ever done to deserve this. Was I really such a horrible person? Sleeping in the car was becoming the norm, not the exception.

Realizing that I was still up in San Luis Obispo, I decided I needed to take care of a few things before getting back on the road again. One of them was finding a bathroom or at least a good-sized bush. At this point my head hurt and I couldn't seem to think straight. I felt so alone. I wondered if anyone would care once I was dead. Suddenly I wanted to talk to Pamela. I wanted to believe that someone cared. Pamela was just the person to do that.

I was surprised to find the front doors open. Heading inside, I found myself in a big recreation room. There were pool tables and ping-pong tables, but more importantly, there was a piano. I guess I was too preoccupied last night to have noticed.

Scouting around I found the bathroom and went in to relieve myself. When I was done, I went to wash my hands and glanced in the mirror. I was shocked to see my reflection. No wonder Suzanne was so scared of me. One side of my face was scraped and bloody like someone and dragged me along the asphalt a mile, and on the other side I had a nice black eye. Looking down at my hands I saw the burns from when my Jeep caught on fire. I was a mess. My clothes were spotted with dirt and blood. I realized these were the new clothes that my mom had bought me three nights before. Now I looked and smelled like I had been living on the streets for months.

Being even more depressed now, I really wanted to talk to Pamela. Scraping up the last of my change, I found a pay phone inside the recreation room, and called the Leonard's. Pamela got on the phone with me and seemed a little excited.

"I know where you are Andrea and you need to stay there," she said.

"Pam I gotta leave. Suzanne doesn't want me up here, and has asked me to leave," I replied.

"No, you stay there. Suzanne's mom is on her way up there as we speak. She should be there soon."

"But what does that have to do with me and how did you find all this out?" I asked her.

"Her mom called me this morning and told me you were up there with her daughter, and now she's on her way up there herself. You need to stay there until she gets there, understand?"

"Ok," I replied nervously.

I didn't know what was going on. Somehow Linda and the Leonard's were communicating, and I wasn't sure how I felt about that. Were they planning something against me? Were they figuring out a way to purge me from their lives? I wasn't sure, but I knew that I had to follow Pamela's orders. I would stay.

I was at the end of my rope. I'd hit rock bottom. I had no desire to live. But for some reason I was looking forward to seeing Linda again. Her voice had some sort of hold on me. It was comforting, soothing. I had to admit to myself that I was drawn to her. Something about her gave me a sense of hope. To pass the time, I would play the piano.

I had just sat down at the piano, when Suzanne showed up.

"Andrea, you need to leave," she said firmly.

Once again I was impressed with her maturity. She wasn't yelling at me or calling the police on me or even staying in her room safely protected from me. Instead she was down here confronting me, cool and collected.

Now I was torn. Torn between Suzanne whom I respected immensely, and Pamela whom I needed in my life.

"I just got off the phone with Pamela, and she talked to your mom. I'm supposed to stay here until your mom gets here," I said nervously.

Suzanne obviously was a little torn herself. She glanced away and reluctantly said, "Well then I'm going to call my dad."

Leaving me alone with my music, she disappeared out of sight. I didn't bother to follow her. I knew she was scared, and doing the best job she could in dealing with me.

I played every song I knew on the piano, but stuck to my favorite...*Be Still*. It was a song I wrote after accepting Jesus as my Lord and Savior, when I was nineteen years old. Yet as I played, I felt so far away from God. I was so different from the person who wrote that song. Still, I praised God through my singing. It was the least I could do.

While playing, I saw someone come into the recreation room from the corner of my eye. Looking over, I saw it was

On the Road to Peace

Linda. She looked at me, and then ran into another room. That was all I needed. I agreed to stay and wait for Linda only to have her run from me.

It just occurred to me what I had set out to do that day. I was going back to San Diego to find a bank. I stopped playing, and headed towards the door. I wasn't going to get my hopes up anymore that someone cared, only to find out they didn't.

Just before I reached the door, Linda came around the corner and almost ran into me. The look of surprise on her face scared me. I just wanted to get out of there, fast.

"I need to find a restroom," she said urgently.

"Over there." I replied directing her down a hallway.

"Good, stay right here!" she commanded.

Well I did not want to stay. I needed to get back on the road. Then I thought of Pamela. If she found out that I left without talking to Linda she wasn't going to be pleased. So I reluctantly headed back to the piano and sat down to play. If I was going to wait, I was going to play.

Next thing I knew, Linda was standing next to me. She had a look on her face that puzzled me. It looked like she was impressed with my music. Was she? Could someone actually be impressed with me?

Within a few minutes, Suzanne showed up. Linda ordered me to sit down at a table near by.

"Andrea, we need to talk. We need to have a plan."

"I already have a plan," I told her.

I could see that Linda was neither impressed nor interested. She rolled her eyes. "I have a better plan," she said.

And so I sat there and listened as Linda talked. Linda was definitely a person that took charge. I liked that. More importantly I needed that. She listed six things that she wanted me to do. She wanted me to move out of my apartment, which was ok with me since I had been kicked out. She asked if I could stay with the Leonard's, until she could find something more permanent for me. She even agreed to call the Leonard's and ask them herself.

Linda left the table and went to the pay phone in the corner of the room. I wanted to follow her to hear what she was going to say, but she gave me a look that left no doubt in my mind that I was to stay put.

It wasn't more than a few minutes, Linda returned with specific instructions for me. The plans were that I would head back to San Diego and spend the night at the Leonard's. Saturday morning the Leonard's would take me to get my stuff from my apartment. I was not to tell anyone where or who I was staying with.

Then she said she was going to get me some medical care. When I told her that I had no money to pay for it, she smiled and said not to worry about it.

For the first time in a long time, I felt good about my future. I actually had hope for once. I was going to be protected from Craig. I was going to have a place to live, and Suzanne and her mom were going to be my friends.

Soon I was on my way back south, and going to the Leonard's. I would be safe, and Linda promised me she'd call me that night. Suzanne had seemed more relaxed, and I felt pretty good myself.

I knew the Leonard's loved me, but they'd never offered for me to live with them. With my history, that was a big deal.

Do not say to your neighbor; Come back later, I'll give it tomorrow, when you now have it. Proverb 3:28

Chapter Five

The Relocation

linda

Suzanne and I spent the rest of the day shopping in the quaint little college town of San Luis Obispo. That evening we were going to put together a meal for her friends. After picking up some items I needed, we headed back to the college recreation room where a small kitchenette was available.

While Suzanne and I were busy preparing the meal, the pay phone in the corner of the room rang. We looked at each other. The campus was deserted with the exception of a few strays that had not gone home. Who would be calling a pay phone in a college recreation room during a holiday weekend?

Suzanne and I said in union, "It's probably Andrea."

It had been a little over four hours since we sent Andrea on her way.

"Hello," I said, hoping it was Andrea.

"Hey, are you sure the Leonards said it was OK for me to come to their house?"

"Yes, they are waiting for you. Where are you now?"

"In LA. I am at a gas station. What should I do with the shotgun?"

"Andrea, you have to return the gun to its rightful owner. Did you throw away the bullets like you promised?"

"Yes, I threw them into a large trash bin at the station."

"Can they be seen and possibly retrieved?" I asked nervously.

"Yes, don't worry so much. Now will you call the Leonards and make sure it is OK. Sometimes Pamela says ok without checking with her husband Arn. I want to make sure it is ok with him before I show up on their doorstep."

I was confused as to why Andrea was so insecure about heading over to the Leonards since she had given me the impression that they were like family to her. Oh well, I didn't have time to think about all this, I had a dinner to prepare for eight hungry college students.

"Alright, give me their number once again." Andrea promised to call me back in about ten minutes."

Arnold answered the phone.

"Hi, this is Linda Edmunds. Andrea is in LA and wanted me to call to make sure it is still ok if she comes over to your house."

"Yes, tell her we are waiting for her," he said with a kind voice.

"I didn't see a gun, but she says she has one on her. She said she pitched the bullets."

"Alright, we'll handle it at our end." His calm manner was reassuring.

After dinner with Suzanne's friends, she and I decided to just hang out in her dorm room. I was exhausted. The last three days had been very taxing.

"Suzanne, did you know she could sing so well?" I asked as we were lying in bed.

"Yes, she sent me a tape, do you want to hear it? She also sent me the words. She wrote most of the songs. She also sent me part of the book she is writing, but you might not want to read it. Pretty heavy. She writes about the drugs in high school, friends who died of AIDS, and Craig."

As I was listening to Andrea's tape and reading the words, I felt a heaviness come over me. The words were those of someone disappointed in life. She was someone who had been hurt, who did not trust, who lacked intimacy and love. The sadness was evident. Suzanne agreed.

"I'd like to read what she sent you."

"Mom, it's pretty risqué. I don't think you will like it."

"I do not want to read it because I think I will like it, I want to read it because it might help me understand her. Besides, I want to see what type of literature you are reading."

I must have read for two hours. I was shocked. The abuse this young woman had experienced was appalling. No wonder her songs were so cynical. Her story was one of physical and mental abuse.

Later that evening Suzanne called Andrea to make sure she gotten to the Leonards safely. She reminded Andrea about her promise to us. We got the impression that Andrea was still agreeable to our plan. I prayed with her over the phone and promised to call the next day.

Just as promised, I called Andrea the next day. Pamela said that Andrea had gone to her apartment. Both her husband and daughter Lin were going to help gather up Andrea's belongings. She said Arnold had asked her to look through Andrea's things for the shotgun while they were gone. She said he came up empty. I had convinced myself that the gun story was just that, a story.

Suzanne and I did some more shopping. One thing about my youngest... she loves to shop with my credit card. We decided not to discuss Andrea and make the best of our time together.

Back in the dorm room that evening I telephoned Andrea. I hadn't talked to her yet that day, and was anxious to see how the move went. Arnold answered the phone. He had laid down some house rules and one of them was that Andrea not answer the phone.

Andrea's new living arrangement, even though temporary, was working out nicely. The Leonard's had a large two-story home. The downstairs consisted of a recreation room, hobby room, and a bedroom with a connecting bath. The downstairs bedroom was referred to as "The Blue Room." According to

Arnold, Andrea had settled in the blue room that day with all her belongings. After chatting briefly with Arnold, he handed Andrea the phone.

"Hi Hon, how are you doing?"

"Okay."

"I heard you went out to your apartment and got all your things."

"Yeah, Arnold took his truck. Lin came with me. I needed to return my roommates car."

I had forgotten that the car Andrea had was not hers. She had taken it without permission. Her roommate was out of town on business and the car belonged to her.

"Are you feeling okay with your decision?" I asked.

"Yeah."

We chatted for a while. I prayed with her and promised to call her in the morning. I sensed she was vulnerable and needed an extra dose of encouragement.

The weekend flew by too fast. It was time for me to head back to San Diego. It was hard to say good-by to Suzanne. Not only is she a fun kid, full of energy, but she also is my baby. I think because of my experience with Andrea, I clung to Suzanne more than usual that weekend. I felt grateful that God had blessed me with healthy, happy children.

As I made the five-hour drive, I had a lot of time to think. I had made some promises that I had to keep. I mentally made a list of things I needed to do. My first contact needed to be with the social worker. She would direct me. Getting Andrea medical care was going to be easy. I knew the ins and outs of state funding, and where to go to apply. I was also familiar with the AIDS foundation, (Ryan White) in San Diego. Whatever I did not know, I knew where to ask. What I lacked was knowledge of low-income housing, and how one goes about getting assistance. I figured the social worker could help me in this area.

I made it very clear that Andrea was not to tell anyone where she was staying, especially her roommate. They did not part on good terms. Andrea's roommate had met Craig once or twice. She suspected she might tell him where she was staying out of spite.

I had to stay focused. God had just asked me to love her. I needed to keep in mind that He was in control, not me.

andrea

Well, I was on my way home. Everything was different now. The tide had definitely changed. Just yesterday I was driving around looking for a bank for the purpose of getting myself shot, and now I was driving back to San Diego to move in with the Leonard's.

I have known of the Leonard's ever since I was a young child. They attended the Presbyterian Church that my family attended. But I really didn't get to know them on a personal level until I got myself into a heap of trouble in high school.

The Leonard's youngest daughter Lin and I had become good friends, so when I was about to get kicked out of school for the last time, Lin went to her dad and asked him to come to my defense.

I met Lin during the time I was attending the youth group at the church. The high school group was called Son Seekers. The youth group was important to me. It was a safe secure place to hang out with my peers that I'd grown up with, in the church. They were much more tolerant of my odd behavior than the kids at school.

One particular evening, at one of the youth socials, Lin approached me. This encounter was the beginning of a special friendship that still exists today. Reflecting back on it now, I have to say that Lin Leonard was and is the only friend that has stuck by me through the years. She obviously saw something in me that none of the others did.

To give you some background on her, she had been a year behind me in school, and attended Washington High. Her mother, Pamela, was my pre-school teacher at the church. I remember teasing Lin when we were younger because she was always wearing a cute little dress. While I on the other hand, was a first class Tomboy. It was almost impossible to get me into a dress.

Anyway, one night at Son Seekers, we were playing a very popular game called Grass Hockey. We played out in the courtyard with special hockey sticks and a soccer ball. I absolutely loved the game. I was a very competitive and high-energized player. I was definitely having fun.

The day before I had to have stitches on my leg. I told my parents that I tried to climb a chain link fence and got my leg caught on the wire. Early into the game, someone hit my leg very close to where I just had stitches. Wincing in pain and letting out a little yelp, the youth leader, Jim, asked me what was wrong with my leg. I just casually answered that I had stitches.

He didn't seem to believe me, and asked me to show him. So I lifted up my jeans and exposed my stitches. I was surprised and really bummed when he told me I would have to sit out the game. I challenged him and told him I'd be fine, but he told me that if someone hit me there with a hockey stick, it could bust open, and they could be facing a lawsuit. I muttered under my breath that he obviously didn't know my parents, cause they didn't have one vicious bone in their bodies. My parents were just not like that.

Anyway, since I was forced to leave the game, I went and sat on the sidelines, next to Lin. Her curious, protective personality took over and she asked me what happened to my leg.

At this point, I was so frustrated with people asking about my many scars that, I decided to tell her the truth. I was hoping that it would scare or intimidate her and she and others would stop asking.

I asked Lin if she knew Sherry Jones, who was in the same grade as her.

She answered, "Yes".

I replied cockily, "Well, her dad did it."

This sparked Lin's curiosity. "How?" she asked.

"He just took a knife and cut me," I answered.

"But why?"

On the Road to Peace

"How the hell should I know?" I snapped back at her. "That's just how he is!"

It was apparent that Lin was not satisfied. We argued a little bit more until the game was over. Even so, after that, we exchanged phone numbers, and promised to keep in touch.

I found myself intrigued with Lin. She was different than all my other so called friends. She seems to take a genuine interest in me. She was popular and liked by everyone. I felt honored that she wanted to be my friend.

During our high school years, Lin and I would spend hours on the phone. I would write her letters sharing what was going on in my twisted life. She was always challenging me to be better. She was what I needed at the time, a good listener.

After we both graduated, we went our separate ways. Lin went on to college, and I headed off for nowhere. After college Lin started traveling with the company she worked for. She had spent the last three years living in New York City. We still talked once in a while and visited when she came into town, but it was mostly her parents who I had interacted with during the last ten years.

Now, at the age of twenty-seven I was moving everything I owned into the Leonard's home, (even if it was only a temporary arrangement), with the insistence of a woman I just met nine weeks ago. Even more unbelievable, was that the Leonard's agreed to this arrangement with a woman that they had never met. It was as if a force stronger than all of us was orchestrating the events.

When I finally got to the Leonard's, they were extremely gracious. I also was greeted with a nice surprise. Linda Leonard was in town from New York City, and not just to visit. She had moved back into her parent's home until she could find a job locally. I couldn't believe it. Not only was I going to be safe at the Leonard's, but I had my good friend Lin there with me.

As we all talked about going to get my stuff the next morning I started to get even more excited. It was all coming together so nicely for me. There was just one problem. The shotgun was in the trunk of the car, and the next morning I was going to take the car back. I couldn't just leave the gun in there because my roommate would eventually find it. So I had to think fast. I needed to get the gun out of the car, and hide it. But hide it where?

Well first thing was to get it out of the trunk. So I emptied out my large backpacking backpack, and went out to the car. After popping the trunk, I tried to slip the gun inside my backpack so I could sneak it in the house. But it was a shotgun, and the barrel was sticking out of the top a good foot. This wasn't going to work. But it was the only option I had. So with my adrenaline rushing full force, to the point where my legs were shaking, I quickly slammed the trunk and walked briskly around to the back of the house to go in through the outside door to my room.

Once I made it inside, I breathed a huge sigh of relief. Now I just needed to find a place to hide it. The bed was almost two feet off the ground, propped up on large cement blocks. And with all that space underneath, it was used as a storage area for some of the Leonard's stuff. I figured that would be the best place. I couldn't put it in the shower because Pamela might check it to see if it was clean for me. And I couldn't hide it in the Avocado Groves behind their house because Arnold would undoubtedly find it, and besides I didn't want to ruin it by burying it in the leaves and dirt. So under the bed it went. Relieved to get that taken care of, I started to relax again.

That night Suzanne's mom called me and asked me how I was doing in my new surroundings. I assured her I was fine. Then she said she was going to pray with me. I thought back of earlier when I had felt so far away from God. I was open to Linda praying, but I wasn't sure if God wanted to hear from me. I hadn't given Him much thought the past few years.

Linda's prayer was amazing. It was simple and to the point. She prayed for God to be with me though this transition in my life. She made me believe that things were really going to change for me. I had no idea how much though. When she was done praying she promised me that she would call me every night to pray with me. I didn't believe her. I really thought she'd do it for a week or so, and then lose interest. But to this day, two years later, we have only missed two nights. And that was because I was too out of it to come to the phone.

That night as I went to sleep, I felt safe and special. I was a priority to someone, someone who was going to pray with me every night, at least for a while.

The next morning I woke up in the mid morning, and after washing my face I went upstairs to see my new roommates. I wasn't sure what to expect, thinking that maybe Arnold and Pamela had talked and decided not to move all my stuff up to their place. However, when I got upstairs, not only did they all greet me warmly, but Pamela had breakfast waiting for me.

After eating, Arnold got into his truck, Lin got into her mom's Blazer, and I got into my roommate's car. Off we went down the mountain to my apartment.

Once we got there, we huddled outside and Arnold made it clear that we weren't going to take more than an hour. That was fine with me, cause I wasn't planning on getting everything I owned. However once inside, Lin was grabbing everything she could. We were very efficient and done in much less than an hour.

Once we got back to the Leonard's, and I moved all my stuff into my new room, I felt good about it. I was downstairs in the blue room, the room I had slept in many times before. I had a door to the outside, and an adjoining full bathroom to myself.

Lin seemed to be as excited as I was. Immediately she started talking about how we were going to rearrange the room. She was talking about moving the bed against another wall, and moving one of the dressers out, and replacing it with another one. That was Lin for you. She was always one who grabbed the bull by the horns. But I had a big problem. If we moved the bed, we would have to take out all the stuff underneath it, and that meant finding the gun. I knew I couldn't let that happen. I was sure the Leonard's would kick me out if they knew I'd stolen one of their guns. I panicked. I didn't know what to do. I had to think fast. So I just played honest.

"No Lin, I don't want to move the bed. I'm used to everything like it is, and I don't want to change it all. I might get confused thinking this is not my room," I pleaded.

Fortunately for me, Pam was there and was thinking the way I was. "This is not going to be a permanent situation Lin," she said. "I'm not interested in changing too much down here."

Well Mom had spoken, and Lin had to give in. But Lin still was persistent on cleaning out under the bed. She wanted what she'd always wanted for me, the best situation possible. And she knew I could use the space under the bed to store some of the many items we'd grabbed from my apartment.

This was it. She was sure to find the gun now. She may not be able to move around the furniture, but she was determined to get out the stuff under the bed. Once again I played honest.

"Hey Lin, why don't you give me a few minutes to get Gus and Scooby settled, let alone myself. I'm a little tired from moving, and I just want to relax for a few minutes."

Once again Pamela came to my rescue. "Yes, let's give her some time to relax, and catch her breath," she said.

Lin agreed, but told me she'd be down soon to help me unpack and arrange my stuff. I breathed another big sigh of relief when they left. Now I just had to figure out what I was going to do with this stupid gun I'd acquired.

After scanning the room, I decided that in between the mattress and the box spring would be the best place. So I lugged it out from under the bed, and slid it under the mattress at the head of the bed. Now as long as I could keep Lin from moving the bed, my secret would be safe. And one day I would go put it back where I had found it. Now I could focus on unpacking my stuff.

Once I put my Scooby Doo comforter on the bed with my pillow and bear and blanket it started to look like home. But it was having my cat Gus, and my rat Scooby with me that really made it feel like home. I let them explore the place as I unpacked the rest of my stuff.

Once I was finished I sat down in my black rocker and looked around. This room had a lot of memories for me. This room had become my recluse throughout the years. It was a place that I felt safe. Hidden away from Craig and the rest of the world I had come to fear.

Of course I had many questions. Would Linda really find a place for me to live? What if Craig found me? What if the Leonard's kick me out before Linda found a place for me? What if my medical problems cost too much? I also questioned whether Linda would stick with me for the long haul. She said she wanted to help, but I had heard those words before from other well-intentioned people. Once the magnitude of my problems became clear, people would bail out on me. I prayed Linda would be different.

God is able to make all grace abound to you, so that in all things at all times, having all that you need, you will abound in every good work. 2 Corinthians 9:8

Chapter Six

The Warden

linda

I discovered renting an apartment for Andrea was not going to be easy. All the places wanted a credit history and verification of employment. Andrea hadn't worked in almost a year.

I contacted the AIDS Foundation and they gave me the names that offered housing for those "certified" HIV. Andrea would need a certificate from a physician stating she was diagnosed with AIDS. I asked Andrea if she had a certificate she said yes, but did not know where it was.

The Leonards had put down some pretty strict house rules and I wasn't sure Andrea would or could comply much longer. It was obvious that she was going to remain a houseguest a little longer than anticipated.

The few days of room and board that I had asked had turned into two weeks. Neither Arnold nor Pamela said anything. I think they knew I was doing the best I could. Arnold made some comment to me that it was easier to have her downstairs where he could keep an eye on her.

I called Andrea every morning to check on her. I also wanted to give her an update on my efforts to get her a place of her own. I never wanted her to think I was giving up. I got the impression from the Leonards that others who tried to help her had given up. Emotionally Andrea was on a roller coaster.

Her emotions were raw. Some days she seemed fine and hopeful and then other days she would be very discouraged and depressed.

When I called this particular morning, Arnold told me that he had a Ham Radio meeting that night, and both his wife and daughter would not be home. The Leonards were taking Andrea's problems seriously and made a point of not leaving her alone. Andrea welcomed the idea that someone would always be home. She was sure it was a matter of time before Craig came looking for her. When Andrea got on the phone I suggested we see a movie that evening.

As I pulled into the parking lot where the meeting was to be held I spotted Andrea coming around the corner with her backpack and guitar. Once she spotted me she broke out in a big smile and came running.

"Hey, you're late, I was afraid you'd bailed on me."

"Never."

"Do you want to meet Arn?"

Inside the meeting hall was a lot of activity. I didn't realize Ham Radio's could attract such a large group. It was apparent that the meeting hadn't started yet. Andrea started maneuvering through the crowd. Just then she stopped and said, "This is Arn."

Standing beside her was a pleasant looking tall man in his late sixties. Immediately I liked him, and understood why Andrea felt comfortable with him. He had a slightly mischievous smile and warmth to him.

"So, you are Linda?"

"And you are Arnold."

Andrea was getting restless so we excused ourselves and headed out to the car.

I had already done my homework. I had picked a movie at a theater near by.

I had chosen a comedy with Drew Barrymore, "Home Fries".

As soon as we got inside the theater Andrea said she had to use the restroom. I was not going to let her out of my sight and she sensed it.

"Are you going to follow me?"

"You bet. The last time I let you go to the bathroom by yourself…"

"Yeah, yeah, you don't have to remind me."

I noticed approximately thirty minutes into the show that Andrea had fallen asleep. It wasn't a peaceful sleep though. She kept jerking as if she was having terrible nightmares.

As the credits were being shown, I nudged Andrea to wake her. She jumped up and looked at me oddly.

"What's wrong?" I asked.

I could tell she was looking around attempting to figure out where she was. I smiled at her and asked her to follow me.

Arnold was going to meet us in the parking lot of the theater, so Andrea and I went to sit in my car while we waited. All of a sudden Andrea started shaking as if she was chilled to the bone. It was a cool night, but not enough to chill anyone to that degree. Besides, she had on a number of layers of clothing along with a lined flannel jacket. It scared me a little because I thought she was in the beginning stage of another seizure.

I turned on the heater, but that didn't seem to make a difference. I, on the other hand, was having a serious hot flash. Andrea hadn't looked right ever since she woke up from her nap during the movie. Her eyes seem dazed and she at times seemed unaware of my presence.

"Andrea, play your guitar for me." I figured if I got her to do something, maybe she would snap out of her stupor. It seemed to work. The more she played and sang, the more alert she seemed.

After about fifteen minutes, Arnold showed up. I could tell that the two of them had a special relationship. Arnold told me many months later, that through the years Andrea had been a pain in the neck, but he always liked her.

andrea

It had been thirteen days living at the Leonards. Everything was going great. Craig wasn't bothering me, and Linda Edmunds was calling me daily and nightly. It was obvious to me that she'd taken an interest in me, and I hadn't experienced that in a long time. Lin was living there, and it was fun for the two of us to tease her dad, talk about romantic relationships, (mostly hers), and all the other topics that girls enjoy chatting about.

But suddenly I was faced with a huge problem. Pamela was out of town, and Lin had a date, and Arn had a meeting that evening. I panicked. I felt safe at the Leonards but that was with someone home. The thought of spending the evening alone in their isolated house terrified me. Arn noticed my anxiety, and suggested I go to his amateur radio meeting with him. I was willing, until Lin told me, "Don't do it Andrea. You'll be so bored. Do you really think you'll have fun hanging out with my Dad and all his Ham Radio buddies?"

I just wanted to feel safe. I wasn't going so I could have fun. But then Linda Edmunds called to check on how I was doing. I am assuming Arn shared with her the situation because Linda asked if I wanted to go see a movie with her while Arn was at his meeting. Once again she saved the day. We both agreed that it would be more convenient for her to meet me at Arn's Ham Radio Club meeting.

So early that evening, we left for Arn's Radio Club meeting, and met Linda there. She had decided on the movie "Home Fries.' I wasn't really excited about it, but I knew she was not going to take me to see any 'R' rated movie. I wondered if she remembered that I was in fact, twenty-seven years old, and had been seeing 'R' rated movies for years.

Once at the movie theater, I needed to use the bathroom. Linda insisted on accompanying me. I could tell she was uncomfortable with me taking off by myself. I wondered why. I found myself getting paranoid. I wasn't sure I liked her being my shadow.

She had insisted on buying my movie ticket, even though I had brought my last bit of cash with me, with the thought of paying for my own ticket. She then bought me popcorn and a drink. I didn't know how to feel about all this attention. My parents had lent me money every now and then, but besides that, I had been self-sufficient for many years. I appreciated the fact that Linda had paid for me, but I wasn't sure why. She wasn't my parent, and yet she was treating me like I was one of her own children. I went from feeling loved, to being paranoid that she was setting me up for something bad. I thought maybe that this evening was a trap. Maybe Craig was waiting inside the theater for me, and he was going to kidnap me for good. After all, Linda Edmunds had just met Arn. None of us knew where she lived, or even if Edmunds was her real last name.

With these thoughts going through my mind, I looked into Linda's eyes, searching for clues. All I saw was love and concern. I thought to myself, "If these are the eyes of someone who is planning to do me harm, I will never trust another human being again."

She has only asked that I *trust* her. I really wanted to trust her.

So I tried to set my paranoid thoughts aside, and tried to have a good time. Unfortunately though, the movie was horrible. I liked Drew Barrymore, and thought I would enjoy it, but it was too twisted. I was also fighting a headache and confusion and fear, so I just laid my head back and rested.

I must have fallen asleep, because the next thing I remember was someone nudging me. I opened my eyes, and saw a woman sitting next to me. She was talking to me, and her voice sounded familiar, but everything looked kind of distorted. It took me a few minutes to realize that it was Linda Edmunds. I was really glad to see her.

We went out to the car and waited for Arn. I don't recall too much after that. I remember getting in the car with Arn and hoping that he wouldn't start asking me all sorts of questions. The evening had gone well, so I thought.

Therefore, if anyone is in Christ, he is a new creation; old things have passed away; behold, all things have become new. 2 Corinthians 5:17

Chapter Seven

The Reflection

linda

I learned that the church janitor had found a beer can half empty in the women's bathroom the night before Thanksgiving. Ray was right; Andrea had been drinking. I was furious and embarrassed.

I asked Andrea about the beer. She admitted she had ONE beer. She said it helped with her anxieties, and firmly denied being drunk. I made it clear I was not going to tolerate drinking.

I was running into obstacles and things started getting complicated. Andrea could not find her social workers number. She had a name, but I could not locate this woman anywhere. I called every social agency within a 50-mile radius looking for a social worker with the name Lee Shafer. I even called her primary physician's office and asked them to get the name and number out of Andrea's chart. The receptionist looked in Andrea's chart. She said there was nothing to indicate that Andrea had been assigned a social worker. I started suspecting this social worker was a figment of Andrea's imagination.

Time was of the essence and I needed Andrea's history in order to know which direction to go. The first day I met Andrea, she said she loved her adoptive parents, but they were not close. It was very important to gain Andrea's trust;

therefore I was not going to jeopardize it by contacting her parents behind her back. Andrea had a sister, but she did not know how to locate her. Andrea did not seem to have any friends and had pretty much been a loner for many years. My brief interaction with her roommate was less than satisfactory and left me with the impression that her roommate was just as immature and somewhat unstable herself. The Leonards were my only link to her past that I could trust.

Arnold and I had developed a rapport the past couple weeks. We started communicating via e-mail. It felt odd discussing Andrea with him, but I kept reminding myself that if I didn't intervene, Andrea might very well end up another suicide statistic.

I started questioning Arnold about Andrea's seizures. He said he had witnessed what looked like a seizure, but wasn't sure of the authenticity. Andrea claimed that the AIDS virus was attacking her brain and he did not know enough about the disease if that was the case.

I asked him about the AIDS, he verified Andrea's story that she was tested in high school as positive. Arnold even said his daughter went with her when she was tested.

I questioned Arnold about Craig. He knew who he was, but had not seen him for over eight years. He said he could not substantiate Andrea's stories nor discredit them. Once while Andrea was talking on the phone to his wife, Pamela, Andrea said she had to whisper because Craig was there. Arnold got in his car and went to Andrea's apartment while his wife was still on the phone with Andrea. He did not see Craig or anyone for that matter, at her apartment. He said the one thing he knew for sure was the cuts on her body were for real. She would arrive at their doorstep bloody and in need of repair. She would go ballistic if they even suggested going to a doctor to get stitched up, so Arnold would patch her up himself.

Arnold said that once she came out to his house late one night with a large cut above her eyebrow. Her T-shirt was socked with blood. She claimed that Craig threatened to cut off her eyebrow if she didn't submit to him. She was totally distraught. Arnold said he was attempting to patch up the cut when all of a sudden she looked at him and jumped back. Startled, he asked her what was wrong. She jumped him and wrestled him to the floor. He said her strength was unbelievable. Pamela heard the commotion and found her husband pinned up against the wall by Andrea. Arnold told Pamela to call the paramedics, thinking Andrea was on drugs, and having a very bad trip.

Andrea heard the paramedic's truck coming up the driveway. Arnold said she regained her composure and ran. She ran to the back of the house and hid. Arnold claims the paramedics asked questions and Andrea answered appropriately. She refused medical care; therefore there was nothing they could do. They told the Leonards they could press charges because of the attack. Of course they did not. As soon as the paramedics left Andrea went downstairs to the Leonard's "blue room" and spent the night. She seemed fine in the morning and went home without much discussion.

andrea

Now that I was settled in the "blue room" at the Leonard's I found myself with plenty of time on my hands. Since I had no car or bike, I was stranded. Besides, I was not to go anywhere with out the permission of the Warden. Arn wanted me under his thumb.

The Leonard's home was on top of a mountain in an isolated area. There were no bus stops or public transportation of any kind. The only time I would have a chance to leave my new home was if Arn was going into town. He then would insist that I tag along to keep him company.

I would spend most of my days listening to music and rocking. The highlight of my day was when Linda called. Even though she was encouraging, I found her to be demanding. She always had a list of "to do" things for me. She would remind me to read my Bible. She would tell me to play the piano instead of watch TV. She would insist that I not drink sodas and watch my sugar intake. It did not take me long to nickname her "Boss."

It had been over two weeks since I moved in with the Leonard's. I really did not know what was going to become of me. Ever since I could remember I never felt normal. I always knew something was wrong with me.

I can't remember the day it started, and I guess it's not important... at least not as important as how I've learned to deal with it. I do know that I was a freshman in high school.

It started out with the Voices, but they weren't clear. It took at least a few months to learn how to decipher their code. At first I wasn't worthy enough to figure it out, but once I was, their messages to me were obvious. Their commands were to be followed to the precise directions. There was no screwing up. You did what they said or else. Fortunately at first their commands were not too harmful, and by the time they became dangerous, I had the upper hand on them. Or at least I thought I did. Sadly to say, there were times when I gave in to the Voices.

I never did well in school. I went to the local elementary school, and lasted there till I was in fourth grade. I was moved to another school where I was to repeat fourth grade. I finished there, only to move on to finish my fifth and sixth grades at yet another school. Then I went to junior high, where somehow I stayed at that school till moving on to high school. That's where the real trouble started.

In junior high, I was in the band, and therefore my parents pushed for me to go to a high school out of my district. It had a well-known music program. That was fine with me because most my other fellow band members were planning on doing the same. So therefore, I went to Washington High. However, it wasn't soon into my freshman year that I started having problems....visible problems. My 'friends' stopped hanging out with me, and to a freshman in high school, that was a big deal. After a while I started making new friends, which were considered the 'outcasts' of the school. I fit in just fine.

My sophomore year came around, and I was having trouble keeping my grades up. In short I was failing classes. Whenever possible, I would sneak away from class and spend time alone at the park. It was my way of getting away from the endless harassment and insults of the teachers and students. I couldn't understand and hear what the teacher was talking about anyway. I just had too much stuff going on in my head.

I attributed my lack of concentration to my drug use. I didn't think that the Voices that I heard in my head had anything to do with it. I just assumed everybody, all my friends, heard Voices. I talked back to them a few times, but my friends just looked at me like I was nuts, so it didn't take me long before I realized that 'you don't talk back to your Voices'.

There were times that I would take a multiple choice test that I had actually studied for, and the Voices would tell me to pick 'B' or 'C' when I thought the answer was 'A'. I would usually mark down what they had said, and when the test came back, I had made the wrong choice. I felt very discouraged, but I still didn't realize that it was the Voices that I heard and obeyed that made me flunk the test.

I remember a time when I studied for a Geography test and wrote down some cryptic notes and abbreviations on my hand to jog my memory. I knew this was cheating, but I was desperate. At the time I took the test, I ignored what I had written on my hand and listened to what the Voices said. Of course I flunked the test. I was confused and frustrated. The sad thing is, no matter how many times the Voices proved to be wrong, I still believed in them.

When I was in sixth grade, I used to sit in a 'fort' I made. It was up the street from where I lived. It was my sanctuary of some sorts. It was under a tree whose branches grew up and over and down making a covering like a small tent. It was there that I felt safe and content. I spent a lot of time in there kicking back and thinking. I pondered my life and wondered what it was going to be like as an adult. I never really thought about what I wanted to be when I grew up, I think the subject was intimidating to me. I had a feeling that I wasn't going to amount to much.

Anyway, one day while at my fort, I started exploring the back yard of the house nearby. I came across a small rusted outdoor grill and some wood. That gave me an idea. So I ran down to my house to get some matches. This started a usual routine. I'd get some wood, and put it in the grill and start a fire. I don't know if it was the Voices somehow internally telling me to burn whatever I could get my hands on, or if I just had a little pyro-manic in me. All I know is that I enjoyed it. I loved to feed the fire and watch it grow and do its flickering dance.

My mom would always accuse me of smoking when I got back home and I'd be in big trouble, but I still kept setting fires. This kept up until the owner of the house found my fort and chopped the tree down. I was very upset. Now I had no place to hang out alone. Still, I adjusted and life went on.

I didn't give much thought to fires for a while, until halfway through my sophomore year, the Voices really got to me; at least enough to get me in serious trouble. One girl, a friend I'd manage somehow to keep from my junior high days, turned on me. In retrospect, I think our friendship lasted longer than the others because of the many years we were in Band together. Anyway, I couldn't figure out why she would all of a sudden not want to be friends. I was bitter that she, being my friend for so long, would turn her back on me. I had lost almost all my original friends since entering high school, and it wasn't easy for me to make and keep friends, especially ones like her. She was popular and certainly not considered an "outcast" as my new friends. I really cherished our friendship and thought she did too. I was so hurt when I discovered otherwise. The hurt turned into frustration, and then anger.

The Voices started in. They told me to get her Biology notebook out of her locker and set it on fire. I resisted at first, but then they got so persistent and loud, that I knew I had to do it for just a release.

So I went to her locker, and got her notebook out. I knew it was important to her. I recall her telling me that in her biology class, they had to keep a notebook of everyday notes and projects, and they were going to be graded on it at the end of the class, and that it was going to be a good percentage of their final grade.

I knew that setting the notebook on fire was wrong, yet the Voices were screaming in my head to obey; I felt I had no choice.

I ditched class, and went to my friend's locker and got out her notebook and took into the bathroom in the Band room. I ripped out pages and crumpled them up and put them in a small metal trashcan, and started burning them. It felt good. The Voices were cheering me on in my head, and they were so loud and realistic that I felt like I was at a football game, and just scored the winning touchdown. All was well. The Voices were pleased, and I felt release. Then a girl from Band walked in, and saw me with the flames shooting up high and the notebook in my hands. I feared I was in trouble.

"What are you doing?" she asked dumbfounded.

"What does it look like I'm doing!" I replied with an attitude.

She grumbled something and walked out, leaving me there with the flames and the Voices. Only now they weren't cheering me on. Instead they were swearing heavily and telling me how stupid I was to pull such a stunt and that I was worthless and not worth their time. Now I felt abandoned and lonely, and very frustrated. I left the fire going in the room, and went to find a corner to hide in, so I could talk to the Voices and try to get them to accept me again.

I'm not sure when I finally decided to go to a class that day, but when I did; I immediately was escorted to the Vice Principal's office. Soon after, my Band Director showed up and told me, "I don't care how talented you are. You got what you wanted."

I was kicked out of Band. I was devastated. I didn't *want* to be kicked out of Band! Music was my only release of the tormenting Voices. It was the only time I could be free of them. What was I going to do now?

I understand now a little more about why the director kicked me out. I was highly talented, but a major problem. On our Parade field trips, I was getting into all sorts of trouble. I did so many stupid things without thinking. I'm sure a lot of it was just purely adolescence, but hearing Voices telling me to do wild things didn't help either.

A lot of the things I did, the Band Director was unprepared for. I think I drove him nuts, and I know I drove him to quit. It wasn't long after I was kicked out, that I heard he had retired.

Well I managed, but not very well. I was constantly truant after that, and I was soon told that one more truancy and I would be kicked out of the school. I knew I needed to stay in school, if not for me, at least for my parents, so I made all efforts to go to every class.

Well I think it had only been a week of attending every class, when I was riding my bike to school, and was hit by a truck. I wasn't seriously injured, but my leg had been hit hard enough to make it throb. I knew I couldn't ride my bike, so I asked the guy if he would just take me home. All I wanted to do was go home. My leg was really hurting.

Upon getting home, I realized I still needed to get to school. I debated calling my parents, but the Voices kept telling me they hated me and they wouldn't help me, so instead I called a friend who had graduated and had a car. She agreed to take me to school. She knew my tenuous situation at school and wanted to help me out.

By the time I got to school, I had already missed one class, and was halfway into my next, which was Physical Ed. I wasn't about to change into my gym clothes so I could jog for ten minutes, which I knew I could not do, so I just went out onto the field to talk to my instructor. I wanted him to know that I was there and not mark me absent.

He questioned my tardiness, and I just told him the truth; a truck hit me, so that's why I was late. He didn't seem to buy the story, but at that point I really didn't care what he thought, I was more concerned about what the Voices thought.

In my next class though I got a note to go to see the nurse, which I did. I figured she could give me something for the pain. She checked me over and sent me back to class. I finished out the day. As I was leaving the school I saw my Mom. She didn't look too happy. The Voices told me to run from her, but I stayed because I figured she was called about the accident and had come to give me a ride home. I was wrong.

She told me to follow her to the office. As soon as we arrived the Vice Principle asked us to come into his office. I could tell that he was expecting us. He told us both that the school had given me enough warnings. They had warned me enough about the truancy. Now I was history. Their records showed that I was truant today, so therefore, I was no longer a student at their school.

I couldn't believe it! I was kicked out! My mom was at the end of her rope with me, and my shenanigans. She broke down sobbing. The Vice Principle used that as an opportunity to dig into me. He blamed me for her emotional outburst.

The Voices in my head were telling me to kill him. They were giving me all sorts of different ways to do it. I debated whether or not to obey them, for they were also telling me it was the right thing to do, and that I would be 'set free' if I did. But I resisted them.

Boss and I have discussed lately the recent school shootings. I have told her many times, that if I'd had the capability of getting a hold of a gun, I probably would have taken it to the school and shot the Vice Principal, and others that I felt had 'wronged' me. She reminds me that even though I was a **'kid at risk'**, *I had something the other kids obviously did not have... parents who were aware of the power of prayer and prayed for me. Boss says that the Holy Spirit intervenes when we are weak. Yet it still frightens me to think what could have happened if I gave in to the voices, passion and anger.*

We have all had thoughts of destruction towards another sometime in our life. However, we don't act on them. They are fleeting thoughts that come and go, and that is the end of it. But for some, the thoughts are continuous and reinforced by voices in our head. It is much more difficult to work though.

Since I was kicked out, and had an 'inner-district-transfer' to begin with, I was now going to go to the High School in my district, instead of a Continuation High School in town.

Madison High was my new home now as a student. The first day I spotted the Band Director on campus. I walked up to him and introduced myself. By his actions I could tell that my reputation at Washington had preceded me into my new school. Even through my politeness, Mr. Jackson saw the troubled youth I was, and the trouble he perceived I was going to give him.

Being my first day, my school counselor gave me my new schedule, with instructions to go to each class and show the teacher my schedule and tell them I was now their student. The prospective plan gave me a plan of my own. If I didn't go to the class, and talk to the teacher, they would not have any idea that I was their student. Therefore if I wasn't their student, and I didn't show up for class, I would not be marked truant! What an awesome arrangement!

So, first class was Band, which of course I enrolled in, but the next three classes I didn't, and then there was lunch, so after lunch I enrolled in the last two. It was perfect. No classes to have to report to, therefore no one to mark me truant. I was free for that whole time period! I was so stoked. No more frustration in trying to listen to the teacher and learn and no more tests to take that I'd surely fail. Plus, there was a large park right across the street that I'd been to so many times I knew like the back of my hand. So instead of going to school all day, I'd go to Band, then to the park to swing and listen to my music, and then I'd head back for the last two classes after lunch.

This went on great until report card time came. The report cards were computer automated so my parents got a printout in the mail that showed my grades. I had three grades for three classes. My Mom was suspicious, and I just told her that the computer probably messed up. She didn't believe my story and called the school. I was caught.

The school didn't kick me out right away, but I was on probation. If I screwed up again, I was gone. And I didn't want that to happen cause I loved Band. It was a third smaller than Washington's Band, and much more family oriented. I had all new friends, with no history behind me, and I felt this was my fresh start. I had new friends, and I felt accepted. The Voices.... well they'd always been a problem, but I was going to make an effort not to talk back to them.

I hung in there through the end of my sophomore year. But it still wasn't an easy road. I was hearing Voices, plus I had started hallucinating. My hallucinations became very intense.

Some were a bit comical, but others were very scary. One of the comical hallucinations was during my typing class. Every letter I typed kept falling off the page and landing down inside the typewriter. It's sort of funny looking back on it, but at the time, it was just another frustration that I had to deal with.

Another time I was taking a test, and the letters all fell off the page onto my desk. I was frantic to get them back to where they belonged. I was licking my finger, and trying to pick up the letters and get them to stick, so I could pick them up and re-arrange them back on my paper. Of course I looked like I was nuts. My teacher came by and asked me what the heck I was doing. I replied honestly to her, and the look on her face said, 'this kid is not worth my time', and walked away in disgust.

My more intense hallucinations were usually seeing demons in the corners, and then coming at me with big gnashing teeth. Sometimes I'd see and feel bugs and worms crawling on me. The worms were the worst. They were long and fat and usually a sick looking dark red. I'd do my best to keep them from burrowing into my skin.

At twenty-seven, hallucinations, whether it be audio (voices), visual, or tactile (feeling things), had become a way of life for me. Being at the Leonard's in the blue room with all my belongings, hidden away from Craig, still did not change the fact that my psychosis went with me wherever I went.

For I know the thoughts that I think towards you, say the Lord, thoughts of peace and not evil to give you a future and a hope. Jeremiah 29:11

Chapter Eight

The Mountain

linda

It was Saturday morning and I was heading up the mountain to visit Andrea. I was excited to visit with her in her own environment. The Leonard's home had been a home away from home off and on for many years. Andrea found comfort there. She once shared with me that during her high school years she would sneak out of her home and ride her bike up the mountain to stay the night. Arnold would bring her home in the morning, telling her parents that he found a visitor in his spare bedroom. I asked her why she would go up there, and she said it always was a safe place. I asked her how she came to know the Leonard's and the story was, as always, interesting.

As I found my way up the mountain, I was amazed at not only the distance, but also the incline. Andrea told me that during high school it would take her forty-five minutes to ride her bike from her parent's home to the Leonard's. I was impressed. She must have been in great shape to accomplish this. It would be a challenge to any biker.

As I drove up the long driveway, Andrea ran out to greet me. At the age of twenty-six, she still had the mannerism of a child. She had just taken a shower, washed her hair, and left it to dry on its own. I don't even think she bothered to comb out the tangles. I had told her the day before that I would bring my scissors and trim her hair, so the first thing on the agenda was to cut her hair while still wet. As I was cutting her hair, I recalled thinking how healthy and thick her hair was, not at all the consistency of a person dying of Aids. I also noticed that her lips had healed nicely after I had given her some vitamin E oil. This also impressed me since I knew that AIDS patients do not heal well.

Andrea was anxious to play a song on the piano for me, which she wrote. As she sat at the piano and started to play and sing I was overcome with emotion. She was a little shy at first, but seemed to relax once she sensed my enjoyment. As she was playing, I was looking at her hair. I was admiring the haircut I had given her. The trim looked good on her. Just then, I noticed a wild strand. Without thinking, I started to move my hand towards the stray strand. Just then Andrea jumped up and knocked over the piano bench in the process.

With fear in her eyes she yelled, "What are you doing?"

"I saw a strand of hair that I think I missed and I wanted to take a closer look."

By this time, she was at least ten feet away from me. She had her guard up.

"Andrea, why are you so scared? What did you think I was going to do?"

"I don't know."

She obviously had become frightened; thinking my hand was being raised to hit her. Her actions reminded me of the phase 'Cat on a hot tin roof '. At that moment, I wanted to give her a hug and reassure her that I would never hurt her. Nevertheless, I knew I didn't dare.

Andrea sat back down and started the song all over again. I kept my distance. The words were touching. The title was "Be Still". Andrea said when she wrote it, she did not even know there was a scripture verse in the Bible that said, "Be still and know that I am God." I always suspected that God had a plan for this young woman, but after hearing her play and sing that beautiful December morning in 1998, I knew for sure.

Honor your mother and your father, so that you may live long in the land that the Lord your God is giving you. Exodus 20:12

Chapter Nine

The Parents

linda

Suzanne was coming home for the weekend. She hadn't seen Andrea since the weekend Andrea showed up at her college, so on the list of 'things-to-do' that weekend, was a trip up the mountain to see Andrea.

Suzanne and I walked around the back of the house where Andrea's bedroom door opened up to the back yard. If at all possible I tried to avoid disturbing the Leonard's. As Suzanne and I approached the back yard we could hear the television blasting. The program had become very familiar to me. It was Scooby-Doo. Andrea loved cartoons and Scooby-Doo was her favorite. Suzanne and I found Andrea on the floor putting together Lego's, as she watched TV.

"Can we go see my parents today?"

Until now, Andrea had not expressed any desire to see her parents. I was delighted by her request. My curiosity was strong. I suspected that Andrea's stories regarding her relationship with her parents might have been exaggerated.

I had insisted that Andrea call her parents and let her know we were coming. To my knowledge Andrea had not talked to her parents since she moved into the Leonard's. I did not want to be side railed with an unprepared confrontation.

The house was on a quiet street with a touch of rural living. The modest three-bedroom home was decorated in charming antiques and had a warm feel to it. Not the picture I had drawn in my mind from my talks with Andrea.

Andrea insisted we go down the side of the garage to the patio and through the back door into the kitchen. A woman, who appeared to be in her early sixties, greeted the three of us with a warm smile. She gently gave Andrea a hug. I witnessed Andrea's stiffness and could tell she was reluctant to reciprocate. We were escorted into the living room where we were introduced to her dad, a tall shy man. He seemed pleasant enough. Andrea and her dad greeted each other with a slight glance and an awkward acknowledgement. On the couch was an elderly woman who was Andrea's Great Aunt Ruth. She was visiting from Illinois. Andrea went over to her and tenderly gave her a hug. It was obvious that Aunt Ruth had a special place in Andrea's heart. Andrea's social skills were not her sharpest that day, so I found myself introducing Suzanne and myself to all three of them. Her father left the room soon after the introductions. Suzanne and I chatted with Andrea's mom Marilee, while Andrea visited with Great Aunt Ruth.

As we chatted, I wondered what Marilee knew about her daughter. Did she and her husband realize how sick Andrea was? Did they know that no more than three weeks ago their daughter wanted to end her life? Did they know about her AIDS? Were they aware of the daily seizures? Did they know about the sexual abuse? I had a strong suspicion that the answer to all my questions was no.

Andrea's dad came back in the living room and asked the girls if they wanted to see a painting he had just purchased. The girls disappeared long enough for me to talk privately with Andrea's mom. I thought it would be safe to talk about Andrea living with the Leonard's. I asked her if she knew that Andrea had moved out of her apartment. She said yes. Andrea's roommate had called her because Andrea owed money for a phone bill. Marilee said that she and her husband assumed that Andrea was at the Leonard's, but wanted to respect

Andrea's privacy. I could tell that Marilee had a lot of questions, but was guarded.

The girls came back into the living room and Andrea wanted to leave. Just before we said our good-byes, Marilee asked me if my husband and I would like to come for Christmas Eve dinner. Earlier I had shared that this Christmas was going to be very different. All the kids were going to be gone and my husband and I were going to be alone. I certainly was not looking for an invitation; therefore I thanked her for the kind gesture and politely declined.

When we got into the car Andrea took her fist and hit the dashboard very hard.

"Damn, I hate them, they are so phony; such hypocrites. They don't love me; they just put on a show for you and Suzanne. I am not the daughter they wanted when they adopted me. I have been a total disappointment to them."

Well, that wasn't the impression I got. Her parents came across as warm caring people that loved their daughter very much, and I told her so. I knew there was a story behind all this, but I suspected it wasn't the same story Andrea was telling us!

andrea

I hadn't made contact with my parents since moving out of my apartment. I was sure by now my roommate had told them I moved out and left no forwarding address. I was thinking a lot about my family the past few days. I missed them, especially my mom. I knew my Great Aunt Ruth from Illinois was in town visiting, but I wasn't sure how long she was planning on staying. I knew this was probably my last chance to see her since she was getting up in age and the likelihood that she would make another trip to California was unlikely.

Boss and Suzanne were going to come up the weekend to visit me. Actually it was really to 'baby-sit' me because the Leonard's were all going to be gone for the day, and nobody wanted me home alone. But I didn't care why they were coming. I was just excited to see them. I also was hoping they would take me to see my parents so I could see my mom and dad and Great Aunt Ruth.

Thinking about it made me a little anxious, so Saturday morning before Boss and Suzanne showed up I decided to do something to help me relax. I put on my taped Scooby Doo cartoons and got out my Lego's and started building a pirate ship. When they showed up, I could tell Boss was a little surprised, to say the least, to find me sitting on the floor, watching cartoons and playing with Lego's. I cared what she thought about me, but this was something she would have to accept. I knew it wasn't normal for someone my age to be watching cartoons and playing with Lego's, but it helped to relieve my anxiety.

I asked Boss if she would take me to see my parents. I could tell Boss was a little taken back at my request, but willing as long as I called them first. So I ran upstairs to call.

My Dad answered the phone, and I think he was happy to hear from me. I was pretty convinced they knew I wasn't living at the apartment anymore. Usually when my roommate kicked me out, she called my parents and told them about it, saying that I was on my way there and I wasn't to come back. But then when her daughter started to miss me, and she needed a sitter, I was always invited back. My parents were as used to my yo-yo living situation as I was.

I asked my Dad if Aunt Ruth was still there and if I could stop by and say hi. He seemed a little choked up, and said it would be nice. I had such low self-esteem that I couldn't even imagine that my Dad was worried about me or even cared. Much later I would learn that he cried because he didn't understand why I couldn't come directly to him when I found myself in trouble.

I told Boss it was cool with my parents if we went to visit. Suzanne, Boss and I piled in the car and made the twenty-five minute trip down the mountain and into town.

By the time we got to my parents, I was so wound up I was nauseous. Seeing my parents was fine. My Mom gave me a hug and my Dad observed me from a distance. Aunt Ruth was happy to see me, but seemed a little reserved. I assumed that she herself was also a little tired of 'my games'. I was always into trouble, and now that I was an adult I needed to act like one. We were there no more than twenty minutes before I looked at Boss with a look that said I was ready to leave. Immediately she stood up and thanked my family for having us over and said the "nice to meet you" line and we were out of there.

Once in the car I was very angry. I was upset that they didn't ask me my side of the story. They didn't ask me where I was staying, or how I was surviving life. They acted as if nothing was wrong. I was frustrated. Didn't they know that on Thanksgiving Day I was driving around town with a gun and suicidal? Didn't they know that I was crazy from the AIDS virus that had entered my brain? Didn't they know what was happening in my life! How could they act so nonchalant?

I eagerly expect and hope that I will in no way be ashamed, but will have sufficient courage so that now as always Christ will be exalted in my body, whether by life or by death. Philippians 1:20

Chapter Ten

The Seizures

linda

Andrea liked to take the bus ride down to the Medical Center to visit me. The trip would take her almost three hours. It was something for her to do during the day. If I didn't have anything planned we would do something fun after I got off work. I then would drive her home. It was rare that the time we spent together was uneventful. Ninety percent of the time I would have to get her home fast because she would start acting bizarre.

Sometimes she would look at me as if she didn't know who I was or seemed confused as to where we were. I started to see a pattern. She would complain of a headache. Within a minute she would get very quiet. She would close her eyes, put her head down and start rubbing her head with both fists. She would forget that I was with her. She would start wandering off. Almost as if she knew she had to do something or get somewhere, but couldn't figure anything out beyond that. Sometimes she would keep walking and I would have to try and get her to come with me, usually to the car, or she would fall down on the ground and not be able to move.

andrea

I can't pinpoint the day it started, but I can remember losing time all through my life. There was the time I was in class in second grade, and the teacher would be teaching us about how to count nickels and dimes, and the next thing I knew, we were practicing our letters, and it was two hours later.

One time I was in the same class, and listening to the teacher, following all the rules, being a good kid... then the next thing I remember was sitting outside by the wall. I knew I had been out there for a while because my little butt was so sore. I got up and went back into the classroom, but instead of finding a teacher that was worried about me, I was scolded and sent back outside for more time out.

I know I wasn't a 'wiz kid', but I've learned I'm not stupid either. These gaps of memory or 'losing time' as I've called it, have affected my schooling my whole life.

When I was in junior high, my two best friends would recount something that happened at lunch, and I would have no recollection of it. I just knew that I lost time. The minutes or sometimes-even hours would vanish as if I had just traveled in time.

When I was in high school, I can remember riding my bike to school, going to my first couple of classes, and then suddenly, I was across town, with no bike, and it was lunchtime. I know I deliberately ditched class a lot, but there were times when I did it without even knowing it.

It was hard to keep up in class when I couldn't remember what I was taught, or what my homework assignments were. My grades weren't the best, but somehow, with summer school to catch up with, I managed to be promoted to the next level.

I've lost just a few minutes of time, and I've lost hours. However, there was one time when I was lost for three days. It happened about four years ago. I remember telling my roommate at the time that I was going to Walmart to buy a Monopoly game. It was after 10pm, and the only store open was Walmart a few miles from my home.

On the Road to Peace

I remember getting the game and purchasing it. I recall walking out of the store and a woman asking me if I had change for a phone call. Noticing that she wasn't very well off, I questioned if she needed some help. I assumed maybe her car wouldn't start, or an angry boyfriend had left her behind. Either way, I was concerned about her being stranded at such a late hour.

I don't remember what her problem was, but I do remember offering her a ride home. I don't even recall where she lived. The only thing I do recall, is her jumping in my Jeep, and commenting on how smooth it rode for a truck. That's it; my memory stops there. The next thing I know, I'm on my way home, and when I arrive, with the game in hand, my roommate is as angry as a hornet.

"Where the h____ have you been!" she shouted.

Taken back by her anger, I respond, "I just went to buy a Monopoly game! What's your problem?"

"That was three days ago Andrea! I have been worried sick! You could have at least called you know!" she said.

Upon hearing her comment, I was shocked. '**Three days**?' I thought to myself. "What the heck had I been doing for the last three days?" This extremely long period of losing time really concerned me. A few minutes, or even a few hours didn't seem so bad now compared to a few days!

I completely tuned out my roommate's angry voice. I had something else on my mind. I had a bigger problem. I thought about seeing a doctor, but I knew I couldn't afford to consult a neurologist, let alone their tests and treatment. I had no medical insurance, and I certainly wasn't going to try and ask my parents to help me out. They had enough in life to deal with without having to worry about me.

What if I had a brain tumor? Then what would I do? No, seeing a doctor was out of the question. So I tried to ignore the fact that I was confused for three days, and it didn't take long before I forgot about it completely.

However, I still lost time. Sometimes I'd lose hours, and sometimes minutes. It was something that I just had to deal with. Boss would tell me something we had done and I had no recollection of it whatsoever. Then she started referring to my seizures. I've always had seizures.

I don't remember when the seizures actually started. I know there were a few times as a kid I had lost consciousness. My parents took me to different doctors and I had some tests run. There were even more inquiries to the adoption agency for more information on the medical background of my birth family, but everything came up empty.

The summer before I started eighth grade, I went to Band Camp. I convinced one of the girls to let me borrow her bike and ride around the school campus. I took off like a bullet and was having a great time until I turned a corner to ride down into one of the parking lots.

At the last second, I saw they had put a chain up, blocking the wide driveway. I knew I was gonna toast it, and I remember hitting the chain and that was it.

I woke up later, and found myself surrounded by some of my peers, and a couple of their moms. The only visible injuries were my knuckles scraped up. They got me up and started walking me back to the band room. But after only taking a few steps, I felt my head pounding. Instinctively I put my hand to my head and I felt a lump the size of a golf ball protruding and swelling up.

One of the moms stopped and felt my head where I had put my hand., "Oh, we didn't notice that!" she exclaimed.

They got me back to the band room, and my parents were called. I couldn't sit up in a chair, so I waited for my mom sitting on the ground leaning up against the wall. I would have preferred to lie down, but my pride of being a tough kid was on the line.

While I was waiting, I asked one of the moms what had happened. They told me I took off on the bike, and hadn't come back. When they went to investigate, they found me lying on the asphalt, unconscious.

I asked her how long I was out, and she said at least fifteen minutes.

My mom took me to the doctor, and I had suffered a concussion.

I had a headache for the next week.

I don't know if that incident triggered anything, or made anything worse, but later that year, I passed out one day in Band.

A few years later, I started having these weird seizures. I would start to get a headache, and then sometimes I became almost immobilized. They didn't happen that often until I turned 21. After that, they started to become a part of life. I kept them from as many people as I could, including my parents.

Then after a couple years, they stopped. I went about a year or so, and then they started up again. After six months of working for UPS, I got health insurance, and went to see a doctor. She sent me to a neurologist, who I visited once, and never went back for a follow up appointment.

Meanwhile, I was getting carted off in an ambulance a couple times a year. I just accepted the seizures as something I would always have, and attributed it to the fact that I had AIDS.

We then that are strong ought to bear the infirmities of the weak, and not to please ourselves. Romans 15:1

Chapter Eleven

The Hallucination

linda

Suzanne, Andrea, and I went to a quaint little mall. We thought it was something we could all enjoy. The Christmas lights were on display and we were getting into the spirit of Christmas.

After walking around for a while, we stopped into a bookstore that had a coffee shop off to the side. Perfect… we would get some hot chocolate and browse for a while. As the three of us sat down, Andrea was very quiet. Her attention level would often wax and wane. This was not out of character for her while in the presence of Suzanne and I. Both of us have strong personalities and tend to monopolize the conversation.

"I don't want any more of this hot chocolate. May I go look at some books", Andrea said very timidly."

"Sure, Suzanne and I will join you once we are done. Stay in the store, do not leave."

"I won't."

As she walked away, I whispered to Suzanne, as I was keeping an eye on Andrea, "I need to watch where she goes in the store. She still gets confused and wanders."

"Mom, have you figured out what is wrong with her? Do you think it is the AIDS virus that has attacked her brain?"

"No, but I do think there is something wrong going on in her head. The seizures and the confusion she experiences, are not right. But, I have a feeling in my gut that her problems do not have to do with AIDS. Things just don't add up. She says she has had AIDS for ten years, which is a very long time to survive such a horrendous disease."

"But mom why would she tell everyone she has AIDS if she doesn't? Why do you think she doesn't?"

"She doesn't have any of the outward signs of having the illness, such as loss of weight, sunken eyes, or unhealed sores. The only medication she takes is aspirin, zantac, and some type of medication for stomach problems. After Christmas I think I can get her to see a doctor."

Suzanne and I were done with our hot chocolate. Andrea had wandered beyond my eyesight and I thought it was a good time to check on her. We looked for her as we continued to chat. It wasn't long before I started to get nervous. I didn't see her anywhere. Suzanne and I separated and started from one end of the bookstore to the other. It was not that big of a store so it did not take us long to figure out that she had left. As we went out into the cold air, we decided to go in opposite direction, and meet up in front of the store adjacent to the bookstore.

As Suzanne and I met up again without Andrea, I was frantic.

"Mom, relax. She couldn't go far. Let's go downstairs towards the parking lot."

I was beginning to have bad feelings about her disappearance. As I looked around the parking lot from the second floor deck of the mall I saw no sign of her.

"How am I going to explain to the Leonard's that I lost Andrea. They have made every effort to supervise her and make sure she is safe."

"Mom, she is twenty-seven years old. I am sure she can take care of herself."

"Honey, she is very sick. We must deal with her as she is, not as we want her to be."

Suzanne and I decided to separate and go different directions. We planned to meet back at the car.

It was about five minutes later that I spotted Andrea in front of a store window seemingly very intrigued with what she was looking at. As I approached her, I could see Suzanne coming from the opposite direction. When we both met up with Andrea, she barely acknowledged us.

"Andrea, where did you go? You promised to stay in the store. Suzanne and I have been looking all over the mall for you."

Without looking at either of us, she pointed in the store window and asked, "What are my Star Wars figurines doing in the store?"

Both Suzanne and I looked to see what she was talking about.

"What figurines?"

"My figurines. Don't you see them?"

Both Suzanne and I looked at each other, not sure of whether Andrea was trying to be funny, or was serious.

"Andrea, all I see is a cabinet with China and Crystal displayed."

"Look, there is my Darth Vader with his light saber fighting Luke Skywalker. And over there are my other figurines all lined up. Look up in the corner, don't you see my Death Star and Tie Fighter hanging down?"

Just then Andrea went to the front door of the store and pulled at the door.

"Andrea, the store is closed! Stop or you might set off the alarm."

Andrea started swearing at the top of her lungs for someone to open up and let her get her Star Wars figurines.

Now Suzanne and I knew Andrea was serious. She was seeing something that was not there.

I whispered to Suzanne, "Honey, help me distract her. We need to get her home before things get out of hand."

Suzanne started talking to Andrea about something or maybe it was nothing. Anyway Suzanne finally got her to walk toward the car.

Andrea was very reluctant to leave her Star Wars figurines, but Suzanne promised to bring her back in the morning when the store opened. Suzanne was hoping that once Andrea got home and looked under her bed in the box where she kept them, she would find them and the crisis would be over.

Andrea's behavior had turned from agitation to catatonic. She seemed to be oblivious to any external stimulus however we were able to get her to the car. Suzanne sat in the back and I had Andrea sit in the front where I could watch her. By this time, I knew a seizure was sure to follow, and I was right. We had a forty-minute drive back up the mountain and I was just hoping I could get most of the travel under my belt before Andrea had a seizure.

We had only been on the freeway five minutes when I noticed her body getting stiff. One look at her and I knew she was well on her way. Her eyes were slightly opened. Suzanne had also noticed her stiffness and was stroking her head, in hopes that Andrea would relax.

Suzanne and I helped Andrea out of the car and into bed that night. We said a quick prayer over her and left. Suzanne and I both admitted that Andrea was a hand-full, but something about her tugged at our hearts.

Suzanne recalled when Andrea was her counselor. Even at the young age of eleven, Suzanne knew that Andrea was different. Suzanne remembered Andrea playing her saxophone, late at night, out in the open air, after everyone had gone to bed. Some of the kids would sneak out of their beds to listen to her play. All the kids wanted Andrea for a counselor because of her excitement and readiness to try anything. Suzanne really liked Andrea and her spirit.

I could tell that seeing Andrea vulnerable and pretty much alone now was hard on Suzanne. Suzanne has always had a tender heart.

andrea

That night Linda and Suzanne decided to go to a coffeehouse near the beach. I wasn't excited about going to a coffeehouse, but I was lonely and really didn't want to stay home alone. When we got there, I didn't like coffee so I requested some hot chocolate. Both Suzanne and Linda ordered hot chocolate also, which made me feel included. However, the two of them started engaging in a fast conversation that was over my head, and I started to get bored. Since the coffeehouse was also a small bookstore, I decided to try to find a book of jokes. I loved jokes, and I thought it would help cheer me up. But soon I started feeling overwhelmed. At one point I felt like all the walls and halls of books were closing in on me. I wanted nothing more than to get out of there.

Once outside, the crisp cool air made me feel better, but I was still haunted by the books coming at me. I decided to take a walk and check out the place. It was a curious little quaint mini mall. Well it didn't take me long to get lost. I panicked and started to become more and more disoriented. I knew Linda had told me to 'stay put' and now I'd wandered off and was lost. I didn't recognize what town I was in. I was afraid they would leave me to teach me a lesson. In the past when I would get confused and lost, whether it was at the mall, or on an outing, my roommate would just leave me. Many times I walked miles to get home.

As I was wandering around trying to get my bearings, I saw something that became more important to me than finding Linda and Suzanne. My Star Wars figurines were displayed in a large store window. All of them were in the picture window. I was sure they were mine. Somehow when I moved, someone must have gotten a hold of them and sold them to this store! I had worked all year to collect them all, and had spent many precious dollars to buy them. I was mad to see they had been swindled away from me. I was going to get them, I just wasn't sure how.

As I was working out a plan, Linda and Suzanne showed up. I was glad to see them, but I was much more concerned about my figurines. Boss and Suzanne obviously didn't care about them though. They even tried telling me that they weren't even there in order to distract me. I didn't listen to them. They obviously didn't have the same attachment to my stuff as I did. I was going to get my Star Wars figurines back.

I tried the door but it was locked. Suzanne finally said she'd bring me back in the morning to get them. That got me anxious, but I didn't feel I had much choice. My head was pounding and I remember Suzanne talking to me and leading me back to the car. I had no idea that she was saying. It was as if she was talking a foreign language. But I could see her smiling at me so I willingly went with her and Linda to the car. That was the last thing I remember that night.

*Discretion shall preserve thee; understanding shall keep thee.
Proverbs 2:11*

Chapter Twelve

The Holiday

linda

The following week Christmas had arrived. All my kids had plans. Jonathan's fiancée's father was dying of cancer and they were going to devote the holidays to being with him. Mark was flying to Texas to be with his girlfriend, and her family. Laura Lee had started a new job and would not be able to take any time off to fly home. Suzanne could not bear that her sister was going to be by herself for Christmas and decided to fly out to Chicago to be with her. Tom was deep in law school studies and would have preferred that Christmas be canceled. I had a cousin, who passed away three months earlier, leaving aunts, uncles, cousins void of the holiday cheer. Needless to say, it was going to look like a very different Christmas. I wasn't sure how I felt about that.

"Boss, I can hardly believe that tomorrow is Christmas Eve and I am still up here on this mountain!" exclaimed Andrea. Boss was a nickname she had given me. I think she was amused by the dynamics of our relationship.

"Are you going to your parents?"

"I don't think so. The Leonard's are leaving town and I would have no way of getting to my parents."

"Honey, do you think the Leonard's will invite you to go with them?"

"I couldn't handle the drive up to LA. Besides it is one thing having me stay with them, it is another thing to have me tag along to a big family gathering. Besides I would be too uncomfortable. What would they tell their family? *'Oh meet Andrea. She lives with us because she has no job, no friends, no family and needs to be supervised at all times'*. I'll be fine. I'll just get a video and watch some TV. Maybe a football game will be on."

After we hung up the phone, I was feeling sad for her. What twenty-seven year old would want to spend Christmas alone watching TV? On the other hand, she really didn't have anyone. She had been living with the Leonard's for almost a month and no one had called to inquire on her whereabouts or welfare. Other than her roommate she hadn't mentioned any friends. The friends she had mentioned were always in the past tense.

After discussing Christmas with Tom, I asked Andrea if she would like to spend Christmas with us. She would not commit to anything. At least she knew she had an invite.

Christmas Eve day Tom woke up with a bad cold. He had been fighting it for a few days and it won the battle that morning. Being congested and miserable he decided it would be best if he stayed home Christmas Eve, and rest up for the next day. Tom suggested that I take Andrea to church and take up her mom's offer.

"Why would I want to go to some stranger's home on Christmas Eve?" I asked irritated.

Tom's answer to my questions was, "For Andrea. She needs to work out her issues with her family. Whether her stories are true or not she needs to forgive, and what better time to start the forgiving process than on Christmas Eve?"

When I mentioned it to Andrea she was not thrilled with the idea, but I was able to talk her into it. I promised we would leave as soon as she gave me the signal. She did admit that she hadn't seen her sister and brother-in-law in over a year and it would be nice to see them.

I was embarrassed to admit it, but I was still a little shy about taking Andrea to church, so we never did go. Instead we had a nice talk about what Christmas meant to us and had some time of prayer before heading over to her parents.

As I was walking up the side walkway to the back door I couldn't help but wonder what the heck I was doing. It was Christmas Eve and I left my husband at home so I could have dinner with this young woman, who I just met, two people who I barely knew, and two others that I had never met. As I was greeted and introduced, the thought came to mind as to what **they** might be thinking. Who is this woman that has come into our daughter's life and what does she want and why is she here with our family on Christmas Eve. Doesn't she have a life or family of her own?

The evening went uneventfully. Andrea did ok, although all night she kept searching my eyes for reassurance. Her mom was very gracious, her dad was suspicious, her brother-in-law didn't care, and her sister made it clear, with her body language that I was intruding. I kept telling myself not to take it personally; Andrea had obviously kept them in the dark regarding her problems. I had a feeling that someday they would understand, or at least that was what I hoped.

andrea

Christmas was coming up. I wanted to go to my parents, but I was feeling so unstable, I was afraid to. In the past eight years, I'd always had a car. So I could show up when I wanted, and leave when I was ready to go. However, now without my own form of transportation, I knew I'd be at the mercy of my family to take me home. I didn't even have the option of the bus living up on the mountain, and with my bike being stolen a few months before I couldn't count on that as a form of transportation.

It's not that I didn't love my family, but I didn't always feel comfortable with them. I never was able to stay very long. There were a lot of unspoken expectations that I knew I couldn't live up to. The Voices would start telling me that I was a loser. I would then fear that my family would read my mind or hear what the Voices were saying. The thought would make me anxious to the point of getting nauseous. I also realized that if I got too anxious I had a good chance of getting disoriented or having a seizure. That would have been the worst. The whole situation created an environment of anxiety for me.

When Christmas Eve arrived, I got a call from Boss saying that Tom was sick and that she was open for the evening. If I wanted to see my family, she was willing to take me. Feeling secure that I could leave when I needed to, I said I would go.

I wanted to bring something that would help me out. I packed my jeans jacket that Michael W. Smith signed and the video of the song he wrote for me. I figured that it would help me to break the ice, and I needed all the help I could get. As long as I had something to focus on, I figured I'd be okay. I also found a cassette tape with a recording of my sister and me singing "This Little Light of Mine" when we were only three and five years old. I thought every one would enjoy it, especially my sister. I wanted to show up with some sort of gift for her, as I knew she'd have one for me.

My plan worked out perfectly. Trina loved the music and was almost on the verge of tears. Then showing off my jacket and the song made me feel very important. My whole family knew that I'd listened to Michael for years. In fact since 1981 when I was only ten years old. I was his biggest fan, and I wanted to show them the pictures of him and I when I met him, and have them listen to the song that he wrote for me.

After we were all done eating, I started giving Boss the sign that I was ready to go. Trina sensing we were about to leave and went and got her present for me. Soon after we were out the door.

It was a pleasant experience. Boss seemed to make things easier to handle. She had a way of keeping not only me relaxed, but also others around her. She interacted with my family very well. I could tell that my mom especially liked her. My trust in Boss was growing. I was learning very quickly that I could depend on her to read me and respond calmly and appropriately.

Lest mine enemy say, I have prevailed against him...but I have trusted in thy mercy, my heart shall rejoice in my salvation. Psalm 13:5-6

Chapter Thirteen

The Appointment

linda

I made an appointment at the AIDS clinic. The clinic was located next door to the hospital I worked. It would make it convenient for me just in case Andrea needed comprehensive care. I had convinced Andrea that she needed to get an AIDS certificate in order for her to get funding. With funding she could get housing. That appealed to her. Staying with the Leonard's was working out nicely, but she was feeling uncomfortable, thinking she might have overstayed her welcome.

Andrea got on the bus and met me at work. We first went to get a bite to eat before walking over to the clinic. I could tell that she was in a good mood. It was obvious that she enjoyed my company. Andrea was a great storyteller and always had a story to tell. Today she was full of them.

Once in the clinic I could see that her mood was changing. She was getting anxious. It took all that was in me to keep her calm. I joked with her. I tried to distract her by asking her what she would like to do over the upcoming weekend. I even brought up the subject again of her cat and rat... Yuck!

We did not fit the stereotype in the waiting room that day. Across from me were two men. It was obviously that one was very sick, and the other was his partner. On the other side of the room was what I would guess a mother and son. The woman looked tired and the son was well into his illness. Next to us were two men, who neither looked ill, but looked distressed. Needless to say, we looked out of place. Andrea was wearing a pair of jeans that looked three times her size. She had on two T-shirts, a large plaid jacket, oversize tennis shoes, and sporting a baseball cap. If that wasn't enough to attract attention, she had with her a large camping backpack and a guitar. She certainly did not look her age. Instead of twenty-seven, she looked fifteen. I on the other hand, had on a pair of tailored wool slacks, silk sweater, pumps and a strand of pearls to complete my ensemble. Andrea and I, needless to say, attracted some curious onlookers.

The nurse finally came out and called Andrea's name. Andrea insisted on going in by herself. It was no more than three minutes when I saw her poking her head out the door she entered, and motions me to come.

"I want you with me Boss."

Once in the exam room, the first professional to interview Andrea, was a caseworker. He asked all sorts of questions. He was trying to determine what her needs were. After he left the room, a Resident walked in. His questions related to her health. Every symptom he inquired about, she had. She was very knowledgeable and used medical terms that even I was unfamiliar with. As he was questioning her, I was focused on watching his face. I figured he was in his third year of residency. Once done, he excused himself and said he would be right back. About five minutes later he walked back in and introduced us to the Attending Physician on staff, Dr. Lou. He started in with a few questions of his own. He looked about thirty and I suspected that he was fresh out of residency himself. During his questioning, I caught the two physicians looking at each other as if to say, *"Gee, this is what we went to Medical School for. We got ourselves a real challenge... Young female with a history of HIV for ten years, has all the symptoms and seems to be defying all the textbook odds."*

Dr. Lou looked towards me and motioned for me to step outside the exam room. I could tell he wanted to speak to me alone.

"How are you related to Andrea?"

"Well, it's a long story. Let's just say I am her surrogate mom. She fell into my life about eight weeks ago."

"I would like to be her doctor, and oversee her care", the young physician said with a gleam in his eyes.

"I will have to first check with Andrea, but she seems to like you, so I think it will work out."

"Great. I would like to run some tests today if that is alright."

I quickly responded, "That's fine. Matter fact I want you to run every test possible. I want you to run an HIV test and any other test in order for me to know what I am dealing with. I want to know if there are any drugs in her system."

I told him I would pay for whatever tests were appropriate. I didn't care what it cost. I needed to know.

After the meeting with Dr. Lou, I went back in to see how Andrea was doing. The resident excused himself when I walked in.

"How you doing kiddo?"

"Ok, the doctor asked how you and I knew each other other. I told him that you were my mom. He looked surprised, so I asked him if it was your pearls that threw him off."

Andrea had a great sense of humor that I relied on during many of the tough times ahead.

andrea

The day came that I was supposed to go downtown and meet Boss for an appointment at the AIDS clinic. I wasn't thrilled about going, but I was glad at least Boss was going to be with me. I hated seeing any doctor. I didn't trust them. I never knew what kind of medicines they would try to push on me, or if they would want blood. And the peeing in a cup thing never appealed to me. Why would they want to mess with a bodily fluid as disgusting as that?

The plan was that Arnold would take me to the Transit Center and I would take the bus down to the Medical Center and meet Boss. The bus ride was ok. It took me two hours to get to where I needed to be.

To pass the time I tried to read, but I was having a hard time concentrating. I pulled out my CD player from my backpack and tried to listen to music. Nothing seemed to relax me. I was anxious therefore nothing was enjoyable.

The ride to the Transit Center wasn't easy. At times Arnold drove me nuts. He always had questions, and today he was full of them. I think I hurt his feelings though because I did not want to talk. The Voices in my head were screaming in my ears, making it difficult to even hear what he was saying. Poor Arnold, he really had been good to me and all he wanted to do was talk.

The time he came to my rescue in high school will always be close to my heart. It started when I got myself in deep trouble with a girl named Julie. Julie had played the flute along side me in Band. One day she came up to me and took an interest in what I was reading. I'd written Lin a letter the night before and was reading it over as I waited for Band to start.

"What are you reading?" she asked inquisitively.

"A very personal letter to my best friend," I replied proudly.

"I've never heard you mention a best friend, or seen you with anyone."

"My best friend's name is Lin and she goes to Washington High."

"How long have you been friends?"

"We just recently became best friends, but I have known Lin pretty much my whole life."

Julie seemed satisfied with my explanation and went on to boldly ask me what really happened to my leg the day Mr. Jackson took me to the nurse's office.

The incident she was referring to was the day after Craig had cut my leg. It was my first major deep cut. It was on my left calf. I looked for some band-aids at home and came up empty, so I decided scotch tape would have to do for the time being. I carefully tried to pull the skin together and tape it closed.

That morning as I was sitting in Band practicing, I could feel the blood start to run down my leg and pool in my sock and shoe. I remember the ones sitting behind me commenting quietly on my growing bloody jeans, but I tried to ignore them. It wasn't easy with the Voices in my head either. They were telling me that everybody saw the cut on my leg, even through my jeans. So hiding it wasn't going to do me any good.

After making it through Band, and having Guitar as my next class, I realized I needed to do something about the cut. The scotch tape I put on had come loose. I decided to stay after and casually walk into Mr. Jackson's office and request a band-aid. When I asked him, he asked why. I lifted up my jeans, and placed my leg up on his desk, facing my calf up, I showed him. It didn't even occur to me that he would be bothered, but when he saw my calf, with the muscle flexing through my leg, he freaked out. First he pulled out his note pad to give me a pass to go see the nurse. Then he glanced at my leg again, and muttered, "jimminy crickets!" as he threw the pad on his desk. I questioned what he was doing, and he said he was personally going to escort me to the nurse's office. I guess he knew me pretty well, because I probably wouldn't have gone even with the pass. If he were making such a fuss about my leg, what would the nurse do?

As we were walking to the office I started to panic. All I wanted was a band-aid, but I knew that it required much more. The nurse would probably want answers, and insist I go see a doctor to get stitched up. Mr. Jackson broke my train of thought by asking me if I could walk on it.

"Yes, it doesn't hurt," I replied. He looked at me like I was either crazy or on drugs.

Once inside the nurse's office, he wasted no time in interrupting the nurse on the phone. He did everything but hang up the phone prematurely for her. Irritated, she hung up, and coldly asked what the problem was.

"Show her your leg, Andrea."

Of course I resisted saying it was nothing, and that I just needed a band-aid.

"Show her your leg," he demanded.

This time when I resisted, he desperately looked at the nurse and blurted out, "She has a huge gash on her leg that needs stitches."

This time the nurse, gently asked me to show her my leg. So I did. She was very surprised and immediately started to work. She put on three butterfly strips, and then called my parents to come get me. I asked her not to, because I didn't want them to know, but she told me that I would definitely need stitches.

I settled down in the chair, thinking all I had left to do was to wait. But then the nurse asked me a very hard question. "How did it happen?"

Immediately the Voices started in with all sorts of noise, everything from chanting to shouting out brief explanations. My anxiety level grew, and suddenly I had trouble breathing and started sweating heavily.

Meanwhile the nurse continued talking to me, but I couldn't make out what she was saying. I think that she suspected she was making me nervous, so she dropped the interrogation. But I still knew that my parents would want an explanation. I had to think fast. The first thing that came to my mind was actually very believable... at least I thought so. I decided to say that in the mist of climbing a chain link fence for a tennis ball, I fell backwards and the prongs gouged right into my calf. It seemed good enough.

I was relieved when my dad showed up and took me to the doctor's office. He is a quiet man which I counted on not to ask too many questions. My mom on the other hand would have been all over me with questions.

While waiting for the doctor to come in and see me, my Dad finally asked to see my leg. By this time, since I had a story, I did not hesitated to show him. But when he saw it he cringed and said, "Oh Andrea!" Then he left the room. I guess it was too hard on him to see his youngest daughter in such a situation.

When the doctor came in, he read off what I had told the nurse, and then he looked at my leg. It was obvious I wasn't fooling him. Still, he respected my story.

Getting it stitched up was very difficult. The Voices still hadn't stopped screaming in my ears and they were so loud I was convinced the doctor and nurse could hear them. I was very embarrassed about what they were saying. They were calling me all sorts of nasty disgusting things. And although I wasn't any of those things, I still felt that I was. Little by little my self-esteem was disintegrating. And it would eventually be down to nothing.

Leaving there, I felt very angry and ashamed by the whole incident.

The next day at school during Band Mr. Jackson publicly asked me how my leg was and if I had gotten stitches. Embarrassed, I shyly answered yes. This conversation got most of my peers curious. And later, when asked questions, I just gave the story that I had given my parents and the doctor. However, I was very uncomfortable with the whole episode. My secret had to remain my secret.

Julie's curiosity made me nervous. I wondered if she really didn't believe my story, or if she was just asking because she really cared. I told her that Lin was the only one I would talk to about what happened that day. I was getting a little agitated that Julie was asking me so many questions. Then Band started and Julie was forced to leave me alone. I was relieved, but still a little curious as I tucked the folded up letter in my Band folder with all my music. Since I was a little guarded and suspicious, and my thoughts were racing, the Voices were having a field day. During Band it was bearable because the one thing that I'd noticed about the Voices, was the only way to quiet or even sometimes eliminate them was through music. But the rest of the day I wasn't so lucky. The Voices were extremely frustrating, and it affected my concentration in my classes. I would be surprised if I learned anything that day. But that was typical.

Somehow Julie had gotten her hands on the letter I wrote Lin, and confronted me on it the next day. She wanted to know all about who and why anyone would cut my leg. I wasn't about to tell her anything, but she was very insistent and in my face. I remember the Voices in my head were yelling at me to tell her, and that she had magical powers that she would release them to me once I told her what was going on.

Under the pressure of her and my Voices, I gave in. I told her a little bit of what was going on with Craig. Surprisingly enough, we quickly became good friends. I really felt like I could trust her, and also believed that her powers were soon to be fed into me. I believed that she had magical powers that would soon be released to me. And I was really counting on that to help me with my problems. However, the powers never came. Instead, what came was extremely traumatic to my life.

Our friendship lasted only a few months, but it was always fun. I think she really was drawn to my rebelliousness and was trying to rebel herself. We did a lot of mischievous things together, always my ideas, and therefore we got along great. But then one day she told me a family secret. Her mother's brother, her uncle, had sexually abused her. The subject was deep and I did my best to be a good friend, including writing letters of support which she did to me in return. That turned out to be the downfall and turning point in our friendship, and in my high school life.

Her mother read a letter that I had written to her, and realized that Julie had confided in me about her Uncle. Her mother flipped out. She was so mad. She informed Julie that she was not to be friends with me any more. Julie called me as soon as she could and told me the news.

I felt so disappointed that I was not going to receive the magical powers that I had been expecting, and that I was losing a good friend. I was so angry that it was so simple for her to dump me as a friend. I immediately turned on her, and so did my Voices. Now instead of telling me that she was someone with extreme powers, now they were telling me that she was someone who needed to be 'dealt with'.

It angered me to see how quickly she made new friends, and now I had none. She seemed to fit in just fine, whereas I was not so easily accepted. The Voices were telling me that I had to do something. I would not or could not have hurt her, but I did want to scare her a little bit. I knew she was scared of me the way she acted when she saw me, so I arranged a little situation that would really make her worry.

There was a girl at our school that was very tough-looking. She even intimidated me, and I knew from a former comment from Julie that she intimidated her too. One day when Julie and one of her many new best friends were within eyesight of me, I went up to this tough-looking chick. I pulled a few bucks out of my pocket and offered her the money to beat up Julie. I told her I would let her know when. I pointed at Julie and her new friend, and made sure they saw me doing the whole money exchange and pointing at them. We then shook hands so everyone could see we had just made a deal.

I had *no* intentions of *ever* asking the girl to carry out my request, and I never did. I just wanted Julie to feel scared around campus, not knowing when she was going to get beat up.

Well my charade worked better than I would have liked. That night when I was at home, the phone rang, and I answered it. After I said "hello", an older, firm, male voice asked for me. I answered him by saying, *"This is she"*. He went on to identify himself as a detective with the Escondido Police department. He informed me that if anything should happen to Julie, anything at all, I would be the first one they would come after. It was my turn to become intimidated and scared. I tried to assure the detective that I had no intentions of harming Julie in anyway, but he didn't lose his firmness and intimidation.

After hanging up the phone, the Voices started in yelling at me telling me that I should not be the one who was scared, that I still needed to deal with Julie. Soon my fear turned into anger. And my anger grew and grew.

That night I had a rough night. I called Lin to talk about it, and felt a little reassured. As always, she tried to get me to think rationally. Unfortunately, she did not know the whole extent of what I was dealing with. I never shared with her anything about what the Voices were telling me. No one, including Lin, talked about their Voices and what they were saying. I already had the reputation of being weird, I did not want to add to it by talking about things people are not supposed to talk about.

The next day I forced myself to get up and got myself to school. I was hoping that everything would just go back to the way it was before I met Julie, but instead, it was going to get much worse.

It wasn't long into the day before I was asked into the V.P.'s office. I had no idea what was in store for me. I just thought word had gotten to them that I'd made a bogus deal with the tough chick. I was a little worried about it, but I tried to get myself prepared. What was the worst that they could do to me? They couldn't kick me out of school on someone's hearsay. All they could prove was that I handed money to some girl on campus. I was fairly confident that the tough chick would not open her mouth and implicate herself.

I went into the office and was told to sit down and wait. I was getting sick of being so popular with the office staff of my high school. As I was waiting the Voices were telling me all sorts of stuff, and I was starting to get confused. Then finally I was called in.

All the preparation in the world could not have prepared me for what I was about to hear. The V.P. started right in on me, starting with the 'rumor' that I was out to beat up Julie. I promptly denied it. Then he went on to mention that the police would get involved if something happened to her. I tried to assure him that I had no intentions of hurting her. That's when he dropped the bomb.

"I understand that you were sitting outside Julie's house last night on the curb with a shotgun."

My mouth dropped wide open. "You have got to be kidding!" I shouted in defense of myself. "I never did that!"

"Well Julie's mother called to inform us that you were at her house last night," he replied.

"Well I wasn't. I never did such a thing!" I snapped back at him.

As he went on to inform me once again that I was to be the first suspect if anything happened to Julie, I started to think about what he said. I started to get nervous. I thought about how I sometimes got confused, and I wondered if maybe I was confused and really did do such a thing.

Then I thought about the conversation I had with Lin the night before, and how she was trying to get me to think rationally. So I tried to think realistically about it, and realized that first of all, I didn't have access to a gun, and that even if I did get my hands on one, Julie lived clear across town. How could I have ridden my bike all the way over there with a shotgun in my hand? I also knew that if I had left the house that night, my parents would have made mention of it. At this stage in my life, my parents were always questioning my comings and goings. It just wasn't possible.

So now my anger was growing. Not only did I now get cheated of the powers from Julie that I deserved, the police had called my home and intimidated me, and now, I was being accused of doing something that was ridiculous! The more I thought about it, the angrier I became.

That day was another hard day at school for me. I was hallucinating and the Voices in my head were relentless. I had no one to turn to. So that day after school, I went over to Rachel's house. Rachel was a girl from church who even though she didn't hang out with me at school, was always nice to me. She never said anything mean or cruel to me. If she did think I was odd, she never let on.

I was telling her the crap I was dealing with at school and with the police. I needed to vent. "I just wanna kill Julie!" I said. Of course I wasn't seriously considering doing something so wrong and drastic, but it still felt good to verbalize it to help me vent out my anger.

I thought our conversation was going to remain between the two of us, but when I got to school the next day, I was immediately called into the V.P's office. They had called my parents, and told them that I was expelled from school, and to come and pick me up. I was to wait in the office until released and picked up.

I discovered that Rachel, had gotten to school early that day, and made an appointment with the V.P. She told them that I had made threats on Julie's life. I couldn't believe it! Why would Rachel turn on me like this? Why was she doing this to me! I thought she was nice, now she was the reason I was getting kicked out of school! I was devastated, and so were my parents. They were at the end of their rope with me. They had tried everything to keep me in school. They had disciplined me, and talked to me until they were blue in the face. They sent me to psychologists and counselors. This was the third time in less than two years that I was expelled from school. There was nothing else they could do. They just didn't have it in them to fight one more time.

Knowing that I was now kicked out of school, I called up my true friend, Lin. I knew she would help to get me through this. I didn't think that she would get me back into school, but I knew that she would help me to deal with the situation.

Little did I know that after she hung up the phone she went to her dad and asked him to fight for me. Years later, Arnold would tell me that Lin came to him with tears in her eyes, begging him to do something. At the time he said things were rough between the two of them. He felt that he and his daughter were growing apart. He agreed to help me, in hopes that it would actually help their relationship.

So Arn went on to request a meeting with the Escondido Union School Board. His defense was that I hadn't done anything severely wrong and that I was being expelled unfairly.

On the Road to Peace

My Dad, Arnold and I showed up at the meeting. Arnold fought with all he had, and won. I was reinstated back in school that day. I never had anyone outside my family come to bat for me the way Arn did for me. So, no matter how much he irritated me today; I love him. He will always be my hero.

My walk down memory lane ended as the bus was pulling into the Medical Center. The ride proved to be even longer than I imagine. As the bus was approaching, I could see Boss waiting for me with a smile and a wave. Easy for her to be happy, she wasn't about to get probed and poked by a doctor.

Once in the exam room, I started to really get anxious. I had to remind myself that I had all my important stuff with me. In my backpack I had a change of clothes, deodorant, my music and headphones, my new Bible, and all the letters and songs that were important to me. Also, most importantly, Pickles, my blanket and my Spiderman cap. I just had to have these things with me when I traveled.

Looking around, I saw so many sick people, and I was afraid for them and myself. I wasn't sure what to expect when seeing the doctor with Boss. I knew she had a plan and a lot of questions. I was sure this wasn't going to be just a check up with her at the wheel.

Thinking of this, I decided maybe I should go in alone. I figured I had a better chance of making it out sooner. So when I was called, I told her I'd call her if I needed her. It didn't take any longer than the nurse to take my temperature, pulse and weight, before I poked my head around the corner and called for Boss. I needed her with me. I was too scared to do it alone.

Once we were in a waiting room, I tried to keep myself busy. I even played my guitar and sang. Finally the doctor came in and started asking questions. I knew I'd been pretty sick, and I figured since I was having so many 'crazy like' symptoms, I'd better speak up. Only he didn't ask me about the demons or the Voices. He only asked me about my neck down. I answered all his questions the best I could, and as I did, I could see Boss shifting in her chair as if she was doing her best to keep her mouth shut (which I have learned is very hard for her).

The doctor left, and returned with another doctor. The new doc asked me relatively the same questions. Not pleased with all this attention, I started getting a little suspicious. Finally one of the doctors left and motioned for Boss to follow him.

Now I was really paranoid. What were they talking about? Were they saying I have to be admitted to the hospital? Was Boss telling him about Ralph's or the night at her church? Was she trying to dump me off on these guys and just leave me here at the clinic? I wasn't sure. Would I be given some new medicine that was really poison? I was afraid. Very afraid.

I thought back to how Boss had told me that all I needed to do was trust her. Okay. I'll just trust her. She wasn't going to hurt me. I just had to trust her.

The doctor that remained with me must have sensed my fear because he tried to calm me down. "How do you know her?" he asked me.

Not sure how to respond, I said, "She's my mom." After he looked at me puzzled, I asked him if it was her pearls that threw him off.

Next he tried to get me to play my guitar for him, but I refused. I wasn't sure what he wanted, and I wasn't going to give him any more information or satisfaction than necessary. He made me too nervous.

After a few minutes, Boss came back in. She had a lab request in her hand and we were lead downstairs to meet with the vampires for some blood samples. After turning our paperwork in, we were told to have a seat and we'd be called shortly.

After a while, they finally called my name. Boss opted to wait for me, so I went in alone. I was in there a long time because they took nine vials of blood. Not your normal sized vials. These were bigger than any I'd ever seen before. I was surprised I could walk afterwards.

When I met up with Boss, and told her how much blood they sucked from me. I mistook her look of guilt for compassion. Later I found out that she instructed the doctors to run every test possible. That was Boss, being The Boss.

He will have no fear of bad news; his heart is steadfast, trusting in the Lord. Psalm 112:7

Chapter Fourteen

The Results

linda

It had only been a few days when I got the call from Dr. Lou. Andrea made it clear to him that she had given me Power of Attorney regarding her health care. It was also obvious to him that she was not very competent.

"Do you want me to call her, or would you like to give her the good news?"

"Am I to assume that she is not HIV positive?"

"She is not HIV positive, matter fact her blood work is one of a healthy twenty-seven year old woman."

"How about drugs? Any traces of drugs in her system?"

"No traces of any drugs whatsoever."

"We have to handle this delicately. She truly believes that she is dying of AIDS. I think we are dealing with something mental."

He agreed.

By this time I was very skeptical of Andrea's historical recollections. She obviously did not have AIDS. Her parents, to my satisfaction, had demonstrated nothing but love and concern for their daughter. The more I got to know Andrea the more her story of sexual abuse at the mercy of Craig seemed a little far-fetched. The Andrea I was getting to know was extremely modest and sensitive. I found her a little naïve regarding the topic of sex. She would embarrass easily and did not impress me as someone who would, or could, allow a man to abuse her in such a barbaric way as she claimed.

I decided to wait until Saturday to talk to Andrea. I also thought it was important that I talk to her in person and that the Leonard's be present when I gave her the news. I had two reasons for my decision; one was out of respect for them, and the other was so Andrea would have the Leonard's to bounce her thoughts off, if needed.

I prayed the whole way up the mountain. I had no idea how Andrea was going to handle this new revelation. I knew that she truly believed she had HIV, and was dying. Why she believed this, I did not know. This was not going to be easy to explain to her. Your brain tells you when your leg is broken, but what tells you when your brain is broken? I was afraid that she might not believe me, thinking I was just trying to protect her. I made sure I had the written results with me as verification.

When I arrived I could tell that Arnold, Pamela and Andrea had been anxiously waiting for me. I purposely did not tell the Leonard's the purpose of my visit.

We all gathered in the living room. Andrea sat next to Pamela on the large couch as I seated myself on the adjacent love seat. Arnold pulled up a chair from the dining room table and sat directly across from me. All were looking at me very inquisitively. I could tell Arnold did not like not knowing what I was up to. I didn't blame him or Pamela for feeling ill at ease. Three months ago, their lives were quiet and uncomplicated. Now, they had a twenty-seven year old living in their downstairs bedroom, with obvious problems, and a woman on a mission who had intruded on their lives.

As everyone was looking at me, I started with my well-rehearsed speech. "Andrea, there is a part of your brain that is phenomenal. You can compose, write, and remember details far beyond the ability of most of us. You are by far the most talented person I have ever met. However, there is a part of your brain that isn't working right. Your brain sometimes is deceptive, and that is where you are going to have to trust those that love you. I have your lab results with me today."

I could feel the tension as Arn, Pamela and Andrea's eyes were deliberately trying to connect with mine.

"Great, go ahead, lay it on me." she said as she rolled her eyes.

"Andrea, you do not have AIDS. The blood work showed no trace of the disease. Matter fact, the results indicated that you are a very healthy individual."

I was not sure how she was going to respond to my news, but I was not prepared for her strong reaction. With anger in her eyes, like I had never seen before, she looked at Pamela and Arnold and shouted, "He got to the lab. Craig got to the lab and had the results changed." Just then she jumped up and ran down the stairs, hitting the wall repeatedly all the way down. We could hear doors opening and slamming as the profanity flowed freely out of her mouth.

Both Arnold and Pamela were speechless. For a few seconds they were stunned, not with Andrea's reaction, but with my news.

Pamela looked at me bewildered, "Well, if she doesn't have AIDS, what is wrong with her?"

Before I could answer Arnold slowly got up and left. I assumed he was headed down the stairs after Andrea.

"Pamela, I believe she is suffering from some sort of mental illness. She is out of touch with reality. She honesty thinks she has AIDS and that Craig is very powerful; powerful enough to have the lab change the results. At this point in her life, everything is centering around Craig."

For the last month or so I was fairly convinced that Craig was also a delusion. I decided not to say anything at this time about my suspicions. I felt it was better to deal with one issue at a time. Besides I knew that I needed to go talk to Andrea, so I excused myself and went downstairs. Andrea had gone out to the back porch and had her back in a corner. Arnold was standing some distance away from her, trying to calm her down.

"Arn, let me talk to her."

Arnold gave me a look as if to say, *are you sure you want to be alone with her?* I knew that if I didn't confront her now, I might not get the chance again. I had worked too hard the last three months on our relationship. I didn't want it to end like this.

"Honey, why are you so mad? This is good news."

"Get the f___ out of my life. Why are you screwing with my head?"

"Please Andrea, listen to me. I know you truly believe that you have AIDS, but you have to trust me when I say you don't. The lab tests are correct."

Andrea was glaring at me as I was trying so hard to remain calm. I was scared. She looked like a wild animal that any moment was going to bounce on me.

I prayed silently, "Please God, I need to know you are here. I am way over my head."

"Just get out of here," Andrea hollered.

By this time I was overwhelmed. I decided that maybe she needed some space. After all, I had just told her that what she had believed the last ten years about herself was not true. It had to be unsettling. She had Pamela and Arnold to help her through this. I decided I would go home and call her later after she had time to calm down.

As I turned and took a few steps towards the back door Andrea yelled out, "How dare you? Who do you think you are waltzing into my life and f___ing with my head."

That stopped me in my tracks. I immediately turned around and with tears welling up in my eyes I lashed back. "How dare YOU! I did not waltz into your life; YOU stumbled into mine. I have given you my time, energy, and love for the last three months and this is how you treat me? I am sorry that my news today that you are going to live and not die of AIDS upsets you. I have treated you and loved you like you were my very own child. I don't deserve this."

By this time, my pent up emotions had given way and the tears were freely flowing. Andrea looked at me dumbfounded.

With what seemed like sincere remorse, she said, "I am sorry, I didn't mean to make you cry. Please don't cry. I am sorry. I am so so sorry. Please, please Boss, don't cry."

Before I knew it, we were both crying and in each other's arms. Sensing we had company I looked up. I saw Arnold on the balcony leaning over and looking at us in bewilderment. I later learned that in all the years they had known Andrea, they had never seen her cry or submissive. She presented herself as a tough kid not needing intimacy with anyone. She never allowed them to touch her, much less hug her. I knew then that God WAS there that afternoon, using me to break the angry spirit of a troubled young woman.

andrea

I had taken the bus downtown to meet up with Boss after she got off work. I was very pleased to spend some time with her just hanging out. Most of our time together was either sitting in a clinic, grocery shopping, or on one of her missions. After our time together, we met the Leonard's at the mall in Escondido since they were in town for the evening. That way Boss didn't have to drive me all they way up the mountain. When we said goodbye, she told me she'd be up to see me in the morning. I was curious, but happy. Little did I know what she had in store for me. It would totally change my life.

Early Saturday morning, I went upstairs to have breakfast. I was excited about Boss coming to see me. But once upstairs that all changed. Pamela asked me if I would clean up the living room, which I was fine with, but the urgency made me curious. Pamela wanted me to straighten up the living room because Linda was coming over to talk to us. I wasn't sure what it was about, but with the Leonard's acting so differently, I suspected it wasn't good. I wondered if they'd found the shotgun and I was going to be asked to leave their home. I couldn't be sure of anything, except that I was getting anxious.

The Voices were telling me I'd blown it and that if I wanted to get out alive I'd better get the shotgun and 'take care' of everybody at the meeting. Of course I wasn't going to obey them, however the rhetoric wasn't easy to ignore. With them screaming in my head, by the time Boss got there, I was jumping out of my skin.

We all sat down in the living room, and Boss started talking. It seemed to me like she was talking gibberish. She was saying something about my brain being talented and phenomenal, but then again that it wasn't working right. I was desperate to understand what she was saying, but I was getting confused. I knew it was important and I wanted to hear what she was trying to tell me, because I knew it was big, whatever it was.

When she said she got my test results back from the lab, I got really scared. I knew it must be really bad for her to drive all the way out to the Leonard's to break it to me. But instead she said something that didn't make sense. She said there were no traces of HIV in my body whatsoever! Instantly I knew what had happened. Craig had gotten to the Lab! The results had been tampered with.

I was furious. I jumped up and ran downstairs kicking and slamming the doors as I went. I was obviously not safe here, and Boss obviously could not be trusted. How dare she! Did she actually think she could fool the Leonard's and I into thinking that I wasn't sick! I knew she was lying. She must be in it with Craig. Of course, it all made sense now. Moving me out of my apartment and in with the Leonard's, only to find me a new place to live that only her and Craig would know about!

Pacing my room like a caged animal, I went outside. Seconds later Arn came around the corner trying to calm me down. I yelled my suspicions to him as he tried to get me contained.

Then Boss showed up, and wanted to talk to me. I was so mad I didn't even want to look at her much less hear what she had to say. There was nothing she could say that would change how I was feeling. She had just taken away my life. Stuff I had believed, she was trying to convince me otherwise. What right did she have?

After striking my fist on the wall, and letting loose some profanity, Boss turned around and started to walk away. I still had more to say, but before I was done she turned back around and interrupted me. With tears streaming down her face she told me off. I had never seen Boss so emotional. Instantly, I felt remorseful. She had accepted me unconditionally like no one had ever had before. She said she had treated me like I was one of her very own. It was true, she had. To my surprise tears started filling up my own eyes. Without making a conscious decision, I stepped towards her and reached out. She moved towards me and gently took me in her arms. We both embraced.

That moment was a turning point in our relationship. God had just revealed Himself to me by giving me the gift of a true friend.

Wherefore be not unwise, but understanding what the will of the Lord is. Ephesians 5:17

Chapter Fifteen

The Holistic Doc

linda

I had heard of a holistic physician in Los Angeles that used "remedies" to promote healing. He came highly recommended as a nationally renowned physician who practices holistic medicine. Holistic Medicine is the process of natural healing by cleansing of the body. Since Andrea was very much against "drugs", she said she was willing to give it a try. I figured it couldn't hurt. Her diet had been so poor the last year; I knew that her system needed some cleaning out. The amount of aspirins she took daily for her headaches was enough to throw her system off.

I made the appointment for Andrea to see Dr. Easton. He was located about hundred and twenty miles away, close to where her sister Trina lived.

As the day for the appointment was approaching, Andrea started having second thoughts. I promised to make it a fun day. I told her that I had taken the day off and suggested we have lunch with her sister while in the area. The thought of visiting her sister and a road trip did appeal to her.

It was 8:30 a.m. I could already tell it was going to be a beautiful day. I had called Andrea to let her know I was on my way. I wanted to make sure she was out of bed and getting ready. Andrea had contacted her sister and we planned to have lunch. Andrea had always admired Trina, yet they were not close. I knew that Andrea wanted a closer relationship. She was learning how to use e-mail, and found it non-threatening to correspond in this manner. I encouraged her to e-mail her sister and let her in on what was going on in her life. I also believed that Andrea needed to resolve some of her issues with her family in order to begin her own physical healing.

When I arrived, Andrea was ready to go. She seemed clear headed and excited about taking the hour road trip and having lunch with her sister. I on the other hand was a little nervous. This was a long trip to take with Andrea, and I knew Trina was skeptical of me.

Andrea brought five of her favorite CD's to put in the car CD player. They were all of Michael W. Smith. As we cruised up the highway, she sang along with the lyrics of the songs. She knew every word and beat. As I peeked over at her as she sang at the top of her lungs, I knew she was going to be ok. The only question to me was... when? I said a silent prayer at that moment and asked God to give me the strength to see this project through.

The plan was to meet Trina at a local restaurant near her work, and later get a tour of her office.

"Does Trina know about Craig?"

"No."

"Did she know about the AIDS?"

"I'm not sure."

This was not going to be easy. It was obvious that Andrea shared very little through the years with her sister. She did say that she e-mailed Trina and told her about losing time and getting confused. At this point I wasn't sure what her sister knew and what she did not know. I decided I would keep my mouth shut and let Andrea and Trina visit without my intervention.

The lunch went well, I thought. Trina was kind to me and demonstrated sincere concern for her sister. I did what I set out to do, and kept quiet. Trina helped by not directing any questions towards me. She however, had a lot of questions for her sister, none of them having to do with AIDS, or Craig.

Trina didn't seem to be aware of Andrea's health problems prior to Andrea's e-mail the week before.

"Now explain to me about this specialist you are seeing today and why," asked Trina very inquisitively.

Andrea immediately looked at me as if needing me to explain. "Andrea not only has these seizures but she loses time and becomes confused," I quickly explained.

Trina looked directly at her sister, "Really, Andrea, how long has this been happening."

"Awhile."

'How often do you have these seizures?" Trina asked still looking directly at her sister.

"I don't know."

I was feeling awkward and restless. I wanted to blurt out, "Andrea has seizures as often as four times a day, she's delusional, she hallucinates, she has suicidal thoughts, AND she cuts herself. This is not normal by any stretch of the imagination." Instead I bit my tongue and kept my big mouth shut.

Trina could see that Andrea was getting uptight by all the questions, so the topic was changed and taken over with small talk.

It was time to head for Dr. Easton's office. Andrea became very quiet as I drove. As I was pulling the car into the stall in the underground parking structure of the medical building, I sensed the tension. I glanced over at Andrea and could see that she was getting anxious. I was learning to see the signs. Andrea was winding herself up.

"What's wrong Andie?"

She looked at me as if she was afraid to speak.

"You agreed to see Dr. Easton. Are you having second thoughts? Talk to me."

"I don't want you to leave me here. "

Shocked at her comment, I asked, "Honey, why would I leave you here?"

"I don't want to be committed!"

"Andie, listen to me. You are not here to be committed. You are coming back to San Diego with me right after we talk to Dr. Easton."

I could see that she wanted to believe me. Trust was such a big issue with her. I put my arm around her and told her that she and I were in this together. Where she goes, I go. I also reassured her that I would never make her do anything that she did not want to do.

After we checked in we were told to have a seat in the waiting room. Since I was paying cash, and his time wasn't cheap, I wanted to optimize the time I spent with him. I did not want to forget or overlook anything, so I had put a list of symptoms together for Dr. Easton. Andrea was trying to keep busy. She had picked up a children's magazine and was looking at the pictures. She soon got bored and was looking over my shoulder. My first reaction was to hide what I had written, and then I thought otherwise. What better place than to hit her head on with the reality of her problems than in a doctor's office. She seemed relatively unmoved by what I had written. She did question what "delusions" meant. I didn't want to get into the "heavy" stuff, such as Craig, so I reminded her of the time she came to the Medical Center where I worked thinking she had a doctors appointment. Before I could get much further into my explanation, she cut me off.

"I know, I know, never mind." She said abruptly.

She obviously felt very uncomfortable when I started to explain. I thought she might have more insight into delusions than she was letting on. Or possibly she knew she had a problem with separating reality from fantasy, but until now didn't have a label to put on it.

By the time we were called in, it had been enough time for Andrea to get totally wound up. She had become somewhat catatonic. Her face was very flushed and she was having a hard time walking straight.

Dr. Easton was sitting at a large dark mahogany desk. Andrea and I were sitting in two chairs in front of him. Andrea had her feet up on the seat of the chair with her head down. Dr.

Easton kept watching her. I could see that he was assessing her behavior. I could tell that he was very surprised when I told him she was twenty-seven.

Dr. Easton was of Indian decent and had a strong accent. I gave him my list. It took me some time to understand some of his questions. He asked me how Andrea and I were related.

Just before we got up to leave, Dr. Easton looked at me and said, "She is a very sick child, but I can get her system back in balance."

He took another long look at her and then looked back at me. "I can see that she loves you, and trusts you. You also need to take care of yourself. She is going to need you. "

His kind words caught me off guard. I started to cry. I had been dealing with Andrea for three months without much emotional support, mostly due to my efforts to respect her privacy. Quickly I got control of myself. I did not want Andrea to relate my tears for weakness. She needed me to be strong.

Andrea was very quiet on the way home. I missed the singing I heard on the way up. Figuring she was emotionally exhausted I kept quiet myself. We were about forty-five minutes into the drive home when Andrea said she had a headache and wanted out of the car. As I glanced over, she was already taking off her seat belt. Minutes prior I had seen a sign that said 'Rest Stop One Mile". I asked her to hold on until I could get to the rest stop. I didn't want to pull over on the side of the highway in the dark.

I was able to keep everything under control until I got to the rest stop. Andrea immediately jumped out and started staggering to the picnic area. I caught up with her immediately and grabbed her arm. Scattered about were families that had stopped for various reasons. Some were just stretching their legs and others were sitting at the picnic benches eating their supper. I knew I could not stop what was happening to Andrea, but I could do my best not to make a scene.

Andrea stopped and started looking spooked. She then put her hands over her ears. "Bees."

"What?"

"Bees!" Andrea exclaimed, as she started to run.

I started running after her. She was running in all different directions, as if she didn't know which way was the best way to go.

I figured she was hallucinating. She was hearing and seeing bees all around her. I was feeling a little uncomfortable noticing that others were starting to watch.

We had been running around the picnic area for about thirty minutes when it looked like she might be winding down. I knew she was mentally and physically exhausted. I sure was. It had been a big day. I grabbed hold of her and asked her if she was ready to go home. I felt a tinge of pain in my heart as she looked at me with those blue eyes, looking very vulnerable and scared. Looking directly in my eyes for comfort, she nodded yes.

The remainder of the ride home was uneventful. She closed her eyes for some time and rested. I was unfamiliar with the route to the Leonards, coming south, and missed the turnoff. Andrea must have sensed that something was wrong. She woke up and was able to direct me back to where I needed to be. The next thirty-five minutes she seemed alert and clear headed. You would have never known that an hour previously, she was hallucinating and out of her mind.

andrea

Boss knew there was something wrong with me, and it obviously wasn't AIDS. She wanted to take me to a holistic doctor up in Irvine. I was game to going. I figured if Boss was willing to give it a try, I would too. I wasn't sure what was wrong with me, but I knew it was bad whatever it was. If the AIDS virus wasn't in my brain making me crazy, and causing my seizures, then what was it?

As the day of the appointment was approaching, I started to get nervous. I had a lot going through my mind. I knew Boss suspected I was mentally ill, and all I knew of mental illness was being locked up. Growing up, my mom dealt with manic-depression. She just went from being depressed to being hyper. I could remember as a young child, her being in the hospital, but not really knowing why. All I was told was that she was very sad. I was afraid that if you had to be in the hospital for just being sad, what would they do with someone who had my problems?

I hadn't had much contact with my sister over the years since she left for college, at least not as much as I'd wanted. When she was a senior I was a freshman in high school, however we attended different schools. So I didn't even have my 'big sister' to pave the way.

The problems I got into as a freshman, drove my parents nuts, and also my sister. I could tell she thought I needed to *grow up.* We were much closer as younger children, but when she started to mature, I was left in the dust. I could only look up to her, and hope that I would someday have the same success that she had. Trina was never short on friends. She was popular, and smart; two things I certainly was not. I never even came close, which aided in the separation that was growing between us. I know that she loved me, but tolerance was not in the picture.

The day she left for college, she told me she was never coming back. Now twelve years later, and she was true to her word. Sure, she came to visit, but never to live.

Boss asked me to check with her the possibility of us having lunch prior to our visit with Dr. Easton. Trina thought it would be nice. I couldn't wait. I couldn't remember one time since we became adults that we had gotten together outside of family birthdays and holidays. So this was going to be a special day.

Since I was going to be meeting her for lunch, and Arn was setting me up on email, I decided to email Trina. The following is my attempt to communicate, and her response.

My Email to Trina

A question for you.... As Linda Edmunds and I are trying to find out what's wrong with my head... I was wondering if you remembered anything from when I was a kid and would pass out. We're just trying to piece together a puzzle, and any info, especially past history would be helpful. I still haven't got an appointment with a neurologist yet, but that's how the government works. Patience is the key right. Ya whatever…anyway.

Give me a write back when you can… I'll be up there on the 28th, somewhere in that area, no idea where though. I'm excited about meeting for lunch or whatever…..

So lets see what happens there….

Anyway, don't want to take up any more of your work time…so I better go…

Love you, Andie

Trina's Email Response

You keep asking or referring to "what's wrong with you head". I'm not exactly sure what you mean by that. Are you referring to your mental state of mind/health, or some physical ailment that you are suffering from?

As far as you passing out, I don't recall why it happened exactly except for that it seemed like you were upset or frustrated or worked up somehow.

I know Mom and Dad had you tested at least a couple of times… and I think those tests showed that you were fine….. and didn't you have an EEG as late as in high school that came out okay? I'd ask Mom, she'd remember all of that stuff, or if you need me to I can ask her. I know too that Mom went back and tried to get more info from your adoption records to find out stuff, and I believe you had several psychiatric evaluations by that therapist you saw for a while. I don't know, however, what those tests showed. Perhaps you remember some of this? What's wrong Andrea? Have you been passing out? It's hard to know what kind of information might be helpful when I don't know what *the problem is. Not to pry but I'm starting to get worried but I don't want to push you. At the same time, I want to help in any way I can.*

Thanks for your note and for keeping in touch. And don't let me push you into sharing with me if you're not ready but know that I care and will give you any info that you think could help. And, I'd love to meet for lunch on the 28th so keep me posted as to your plan. I can meet you pretty much anywhere, okay?

Talk to you soon.

Love, Trina

Even though I was anxious about it, I knew Boss would help me with the conversation. I assumed Trina would have a lot of questions for me, and I was right.

Trina had chosen a popular Brewery. I was thrilled because I knew I could just get a burger, fries and a freshly brewed beer. Boss put her foot down regarding my beer consumption, but I didn't think she would say anything in front of my sister. I was right. As it turned out, Trina had the same taste in food that I did and requested a side of ranch dressing to dip our fries in. I felt very close to her as we shared the dressing dip together.

It didn't take long for Trina to start asking awkward questions, and making demands.

"How long are you planning on staying at the Leonards, and when are you going to get a job?" she quizzed me.

I looked at Boss to help me to respond, but she stayed quiet. I felt very uncomfortable, thinking my sister thought I was sponging a free ride of life from the Leonard's and just being too lazy to get back on my feet with a job.

I knew what Trina would have done in my situation. If she had lost her job and her place to live, she'd have a hotel room set up, and start working somewhere new the next day. She just had that internal drive to be completely independent.

I on the other hand, *needed* the Leonard's. I had no place to live, and they were willing to help me out. I also needed

Boss financially since I had no job and not even a penny saved in the bank. I was as close to homeless as I could get, and without the Leonard's and Boss's big hearts, I would be on the streets.

I thought about my situation as I sat there with my big sister, so successful in life, and I became very ashamed. It wasn't that I was lazy... I wasn't. It wasn't that I was a user... I wasn't. It was so simple, but I couldn't explain it to Trina... not to *anyone.* The Voices were so loud, and my thought process was so tweaked. I couldn't answer the simplest questions my sister was throwing at me, how in the world was I going to be able to handle a job? How was I even going to make it through the interview process? How was I supposed to convince a prospective employer that they wanted me to work for them? I didn't even want myself with my problems... I saw no hope in anyone else wanting me!

I didn't want to be in this situation. I'd give anything for my job at UPS back. I wasn't sure if I could handle it, but I was still willing to try. I had the job for three years. UPS fired me when I flipped out and wrote some vulgar comments on a girl's locker, after she made fun of me.

My mind was just so tormented and confused, I didn't know what to do. I was having these weird seizures and losing time, and was getting hints from the Leonard's and Boss, that some of the stuff I'd experienced, didn't happen. That in itself was hard, and then added on to all that, I saw, heard and sometimes felt the demons. I also had noise in my head, and was fighting suicidal ideation.

With all that going on, I was expected to get a job and support my own place to live? I could barely take care of Gus and Scooby, my cat and rat. I silently prayed for Trina to understand one day.

By the time we got to Dr. Easton's, I was a basket case. I was totally convinced Boss was admitting me to a hospital. There was absolutely no doubt in my mind, and I was scared. I made sure I had Pickles and my blanket, because I knew I wasn't going home with Boss.

She could see I was more nervous than an alley cat, and she asked me what was wrong. It took all the courage I had to admit my fear. I told her I didn't want to be committed. I could see my response almost brought her to tears. She tried to reassure me that there was no way she was leaving there without me. But try as she did, there was no way she was going to be able to convince me. I was positive that I was staying, and she was going home.

When we got inside Dr. Easton's office, Boss tried to keep me busy. I found some Young Readers magazines with pictures. The Voices were so loud I knew I wouldn't be able to concentrate on an adult article.

As I was messing around with the magazines, Boss got out some papers that she had prepared for the doctor and was focusing on them. My curiosity got the better of me, I leaned close to her to see what she was reading.

On one of the papers she had made a list of all the symptoms she knew I had: Voices, hallucinations, seizures, confusion and delusions. I understood all of them, with the exception of delusions. I asked her what that meant.

"Do you remember when you came down to the Medical Center that day to meet me?"

"Yes," I answered wondering where she was going with this.

"Do you remember how you called me when you got home and told me that your Doctor's office had called you and told you that you had to go back down there...."

Quickly I interrupted her. "I know, they told me...."

This was one thing I hadn't told Boss about. I thought I'd had an appointment that day, and that when I got home my doctor had called to tell me I needed to be admitted to the hospital. But when I called them a couple days later, the receptionist, nurse and my doctor had no idea what I was talking about. They told me they had never called me. Up until now, the whole situation bothered me, but I just thought either they got everything messed up at the office, or I was just confused.

But Boss was trying to tell me that I was delusional. I now remembered the term. I'd heard it before... "Delusions of Grandeur." What was she talking about? I didn't believe I was a millionaire, or Jesus Christ, or someone with a special calling. Just because I thought I was infected with AIDS didn't make me delusional. I was just paranoid.

Suddenly the Voices became so loud; I couldn't hear a thing. They were screaming all sorts of bitter things in my head. I felt like crying I was so overwhelmed. The Voices were telling me I was stupid and I was going to die, unless I killed Boss and the doctor.

I did the only thing that comforted me at times like this. I started rubbing my head with my fists. It was soothing, and if I could focus enough to hear the rubbing motion, then I could fight the Voices.

A few minutes later, we were in Dr. Easton's office, and he was looking at me from across a large desk. He looked so distorted it scared me. So I wouldn't look at him unless I had to. I don't know how long we were actually in there with him, or what he said or did. All I knew is that he never touched me, and I didn't have to take off my clothes. I liked that.

However the Voices remained relatively loud until we were out of the office and down in the car. At that point I realized that Boss didn't commit me to a hospital, and it didn't seem like she was going to. I finally started to relax.

When we got back on the road, I felt an extreme headache coming on. I would get them periodically, and they were very intense. I envisioned steel rods, 1/2inch diameter going through my skull deep into my brain. Sometimes I could feel the rods surfaced on the opposite side of my head; those were the worst.

Usually these headaches were tolerable; it was what followed that scared me. I'd lose time, have a seizure, or start hallucinating. I could never find peace from them once they started. I would just have to wait them out. While in the car, I tried putting my head between my knees. It seemed to help a little bit, but then I started to hear bees buzzing. The buzzing was getting louder which only meant one thing, they were coming, and would be here soon.

The next thing I remember is Boss and I in the car and her mumbling something about being lost. I looked around and knew exactly where we were. She had taken the wrong turn off, but was still heading in the right direction. I was surprised that we were doing such good time. It seemed like it had only been about twenty minutes since we left Dr. Easton's offices. I looked at my watch and realized that we had left Dr. Easton's office over three hours ago.

Endure everything with patience. Colossians 1:11

Chapter Sixteen

The Drops

andrea

Dr. Easton was convinced he could help me. Funny, I really didn't see anything wrong with me. I knew I heard Voices and saw scary stuff and got confused, but for some reason, as soon as I was approached with 'a treatment from a doctor', I didn't believe I was ill in any way.

Boss was spending a good chunk of money on me though, so I knew I had to follow Dr. Easton's orders. He gave me a number of 'drops' that were supposed to help get my system back on track. They were little bottles of liquid with an eye-dropper in each. I was supposed to take two drops orally at different intervals throughout the day. I would have as many as six to eight bottles of different remedies. Some had to be taken every four hours, some every three hours, some only at night, some only twice a day. Needless to say I was overwhelmed with the schedule, so Boss wrote down the schedule on a piece of paper for me to understand. She figured out what time I went to bed and backed up the hours in the day so I was sure to take all that I needed to take during the day. Boss had a big thing about schedules so she was thrilled that I now was forced to be on one. She wrote down the time, the drops, the doses, and color coded everything making it easy for me to follow and understand.

Actually the drops turned out to be the easy part. It was the strict diet that Dr. Easton put me on that pained me. I was to eat only chicken along with mangos, strawberries, papaya, and cauliflower. For breakfast I could have oatmeal with my fruit. I must have looked so shocked when he stated the diet that he asked me what I liked to eat. I told him my favorite, *Taco Bell;* specifically burritos from Taco Bell... a bean burrito, no onion, no red sauce, plus sour cream. Dr. Easton said I could treat myself once a week to a burrito, but with only beans and tomatoes, no sour cream, no cheese. I couldn't believe it; only beans and tomatoes?

On the way home from our second visit to Dr. Easton's, Boss told me that if I stuck to the diet and drops for a month she would take me to Disneyland. Well that was a deal. I did stick to the diet and drops and I felt good. My body felt more energetic, my hair became very shinny, my face cleared up and I lost weight. But, my problems didn't go away. I still heard Voices, still saw demons, and got confused. Even after several visits to see Dr. Easton, mentally, things didn't change.

Behold, I am the Lord, the God of all flesh, is there any thing too hard for me? Jeremiah 32:27

Chapter Seventeen

The Diagnoses

linda

In the interim, while I waited for Andrea's visit to the neurologist, I got into the Internet and using my search engine, plugged in the word 'Mental Health'. The next thing I plugged in was 'hallucinations'. A large list of disorders and conditions showed up on the screen. Slowly I started narrowing it down to the symptoms that I had witnessed with Andrea.

I was watching Andrea very closely, and keeping a log. I was looking for more indications of other symptoms that would assist me. I finally was convinced that I had a diagnosis.

Tom would tease me and tell others that his wife was like a dog with a bone when it came to Andrea. I was relentless and determined.

"Honey, I think I know what is wrong with Andrea."

"You do?"

"Yes, I think she has a brain disease called "Schizophrenia."

After explaining to Tom all that I had read and witnessed, he agreed that if I wasn't right, I was sure close.

Schizophrenia is a very misunderstood disease. Possibly the most misunderstood of all the many diseases. Often when people hear the word schizo, they think of a person with a split personality. Movies such as. *Dr. Jekyll and Mr. Hyde*", "*Three faces of Eve"*, or the most recent *"Me, Myself and Irene"*, continues to promote the myth.

Schizophrenia is a biological brain disorder such as Alzheimer's or Multiple Sclerosis. It causes serious brain dysfunction. It is a very complex illness, which is thought to be due to a number of factors acting together. These factors may include genetic influences, trauma, such as an injury to the brain, including occurring at or around the time of birth.

During fetal development the brain begins to make neurons and wiring them together. 250,000 new neurons are made every minute. By the time you are born most of the neurons your brain will ever have are already formed. Yet not completely wired together. As an infant you begin to experience the sights and sounds and sensations of the world. During this experience, neurons fire. Every time they fire, they build connections with other neurons. Neurons that fire together wire together.

By the age of two, your brain has twice as many synapses and uses twice as much of the body's energy as an adult's brain. Now your brain begins to fine-tune itself, strengthening connections you use and pruning away connections you don't.

During adolescence is when much of the "pruning" is done in our brains. It is believed that during adolescence when the nerve cells grow and divide, building connections with each other, the nerve cells in schizophrenics migrate to the wrong area leaving small regions of the brain miswired or with a faulty connection. This causes serious brain dysfunction. Many, such as Andrea, start to experience symptoms due to this miswiring during their high school years.

In laymen's terms, which I could understand, schizophrenia was explained as a brain disorder which impairs ones ability to think clearly, manage his or her emotions, make decisions, or relate to others. The disease produces hallucinations, which consist of hearing voices, seeing objects that don't exist, or holding on to beliefs that are obviously false.

Thought disorder is the most profound symptoms, since it prevents clear thinking and rational responses. Thoughts may come very fast or be slow to form, or not at all. False beliefs that have no logical basis are called delusions. Some people also feel they are being persecuted, such as in Andrea's case. Some are convinced they are being spied on or plotted against. They may have grandiose delusions or think they are all-powerful, capable of anything, and invulnerable to danger. They may also have a strong religious drive, or believe they have a personal mission to right the wrongs of the world.

Hallucination is a change in perception. It turns the world of a schizophrenic topsy-turvy. Sensory messages to the brain from the eyes, ears, nose, skin, and taste buds become confused. As with Andrea, she actually hears, sees, smells and feels sensations that are not real. Imagine you seeing a door in a wall where no door exists. Or having a lion, a tiger, or a demon suddenly appear. Colors, shapes, and faces may change before the person's eyes. There may also be hypersensitivity to sounds, tastes, and smells. A ringing telephone might seem as loud as a fire alarm bell, or a loved one's voice as threatening as a barking dog. Sense of touch may also be distorted. Someone may literally "feel" their skin is crawling, or conversely, they may feel nothing, not even pain from a real injury.

Personality change is often a key to recognizing schizophrenia. At first, changes may be subtle, minor and go unnoticed. In Andrea's case her changes were very subtle. She was always considered immature, and irresponsible; therefore during her high school years her odd behavior was attributed to her immaturity.

It is no wonder that someone who is experiencing such profound and frightening changes will often try to keep them a secret. There is often a strong need to deny what is happening, and to avoid other people and situations where the fact that one is "different" might be discovered.

Psychological distress is intense, but most of it remains hidden. Strong denial, born out of fear often exists. The pain of schizophrenia is further accentuated by the person's awareness of the worry and suffering they may be causing their family and friends. People with schizophrenia need understanding, patience, and reassurance that they will not be abandoned.

Warning Signs
- Hearing or seeing something that does not exist
- Disorganized speech, impaired communications
- Constant feeling of being watched
- Deterioration of academic or work performance
- Major mood changes
- Changes in personal hygiene and appearance
- Self-obsession
- Increase withdrawal from social situations
- Irrational, angry or fearful response to loved ones
- Inability to sleep or concentrate
- Inappropriate or bizarre behavior
- Extreme preoccupation with religion or the occult

Andrea had all the classic characteristics of the disease. I was juggling between two emotions; one of relief that I could now move forward knowing what was wrong, and the other of the sad painful reality of it all.

Have I not commanded thee? Be strong and of good courage, be not afraid, for the Lord God is with thee. Joshua 1:9

Chapter Eighteen

The Disclosure

linda

"Andie, do you ever hear voices?" I asked trying to remain nonchalant.

"Why do you want to know?" she replied softly.

"I think I know what is wrong with you and I need you to be very honest with me."

After much hesitation, she answered, "Maybe."

"Honey, I can only help if I know what I am dealing with."

"Yea, I do hear voices, but I don't talk to anyone about them."

"Sweetheart, I believe that you have a mental illness called Schizophrenia."

She stood there staring at me and then took a few steps back and fell on her knees, as if the strength of her legs had left her body.

I could tell my words cut right through her. At that moment I only wanted to hold her, and tell her that what I just said was not true, and I take it all back.

"It's ok Andie, there is help for the illness. Please don't worry. I will help you to get the care you need. I am in this with you. We can do what needs to be done together. Try not to be scared."

I was searching for the words to say that would take the sting away. Her silence was killing me. I felt so bad for her. I knew she was scared.

andrea

I remember the day as if it was yesterday. Boss seemed distracted and more quiet than usual. Finally she looked at me as if she wanted to ask me something, but wasn't sure how to approach the subject.

"What!" I said breaking the awkward silence.

After a moment or two she gently asked me.

I knew she had something on her mind, but not this. Her question really threw me. I wasn't prepared. The Voices were something I'd never told anyone about.

I decided to answer her as vaguely as possible.

That's when Boss dropped *the bomb*.

I stared at her shocked that she'd even entertain the idea of me being a 'schitzo'. Just then under the pressures of her words, my legs bucked and I fell to my knees. I knew *something* was wrong with me, but being schizophrenic?! It couldn't be true. Boss was just being dramatic. I didn't know the actual definition of schizophrenia, but I was sure it meant I would need to be locked up in the wacko ward for the rest of my life.

Suddenly an incident came to mind; I remembered when I was in my senior year in high school someone laughing and saying, "Did you hear about Andrea Nelson mentioned in the yearbook as voted the most likely to become a schitzo?" At the time I was more hurt that they were laughing at me then the implications of their joke.

It was all true. Boss thought I was schitzo so I must be. What would become of me? My thoughts started racing. The idea of me ever having a professional career was not a possibility. And what about marriage? What man would want to marry a crazy person? And without being married, I would never have kids. My life suddenly seemed to have no future, let alone meaning.

He gives strength to the weary and increases the power of the weak. Isaiah 40:29

Chapter Nineteen

The Disneyland Trip

linda

I had promised Andrea that I would take her to Disneyland if she would stay on the diet and drops for one month. Since Dr. Easton's office was in the same town as the amusement park Andrea made arrangements with Trina for us to stay the night at her place. She and I would then go see Dr. Easton the following morning. Disneyland, Dr. Easton and Trina were within a few minutes of each other making the plan doable.

Andrea was dressed, packed and ready when I arrived at 8:00 a.m. During the two-hour trip, Andrea sang to all her Michael W. Smith CD's at the top of her lungs.

I considered myself pretty fit for a woman in her late forties, but I wasn't prepared for the running around I did that day. Andrea kept me running from the time we got out of the car in the parking lot. She literally ran from ride to ride. It was like having to keep up with an eight year old. I had never seen so much of Disneyland in such a short amount of time. Andrea insisted that she wanted to stay until the park closed at 9:00 p.m. She definitely wanted to make the most of her trip to the "Happiest Place on Earth."

She was doing well overall. There were a few times I was concerned. For instance, we stopped to view a huge marble that was centered in the middle of a base. The marble had to have been twenty feet in circumference. The marble rotated slowly as water dripped down all sides. I watched as Andrea went up to the marble and touched it. It wasn't that she touched it that concerned me. The attraction encouraged those to walk up and touch it. It was the duration of time that she spent touching it that was odd. She placed both hands on the marble and stood there in a trance for about five minutes, as the water ran off her hands. She didn't seem to notice or care that the sleeves to her jacket were getting soaked as the water ran down her hands to her wrists. Andrea was totally enthralled with the water. She finally came back from wherever her mind had taken her and took off running for the next ride, as so did I.

Around 8:00 p.m. I could see that she was having some visible problems. After observing her for the last five months, I was tuned in enough to see when she was hallucinating, even if she tried to cover it up.

"Andie, maybe we should call it a day and start heading out to the car."

"No Boss, it's still early. I want to stay until the park closes."

"But, I think you are having some problems."

"No, I am fine. I am used to it. It's not bad."

We stayed about another thirty minutes when I could see she was having a harder time staying on top of her hallucinations.

On the drive up that morning, Andrea and I decided we would not stay at her sister's and instead get an inexpensive hotel room. Andrea had expressed some anxiety about spending the night at Trina's. She was afraid that she would have a seizure or start hallucinating during the night and frighten her sister. Andrea was still very guarded about her family knowing the magnitude of her problems.

The hotel was only ten minutes away from Disneyland. Once in the hotel room I felt my body start to relax and I realized how exhausted I was. Andrea was like a kid in a hotel room for the first time. She jumped on the beds, looked in all the drawers and closets and went out on the balcony to access the place with excitement. She finally settled down after getting her hands on the TV remote control. She was thrilled that she found her favorite show, Chicago Hope. As long as she was preoccupied with the program I thought I would take a shower and get ready for bed.

The shower revived me a little. I propped myself on the other bed in participation of watching the last half of Chicago Hope with Andrea.

I don't remember much of the show. I had obviously fallen asleep soon after getting comfortable. By the time I woke up, the television was off and Andrea was gone. I panicked. I looked at the clock on the nightstand. It was 11:30 p.m. Chicago Hope had been over for thirty-minutes. I quickly ran out into the hall. I did not see her. I ran back into the room and grabbed my jacket. I ran down the stairs to the outside. Still no Andrea. I ran around the building. Still no Andrea. I was beside myself. She obviously got confused and wandered off. The hotel was on a busy four-lane avenue. She could have gone in either direction. I ran back to the room to get my car keys and put on my shoes. I was praying the whole time. This was serious. If Andrea was confused she would try and contact someone; most likely me. In my preoccupation with Andrea, I had completely forgotten about calling Tom and informing him of our change of plans. If Andrea called our home, Tom would not be able to help. Matter fact he would be worried that we weren't together. If she called the Leonards they wouldn't be able to help either. The thought of her wandering around, confused and alone in a strange city broke my heart. I just had to find her.

As I rounded the corner to the front of the Hotel where I had parked my car, I saw Andrea. She was standing next to my car.

"Oh my gosh, sweetheart, are you alright?" I was never more relieved to see anyone in my entire life.

She looked at me with a blank look on her face. As I gave her a hug I could feel her cold skin. She had been wandering outside for at least forty minutes without her jacket.

Finally she spoke, "I did good Boss. I found your car."

We both walked hand and hand back up to our room. As she was getting ready for bed, I put the latch on the door and moved a stuffed chair in front of it. If she decides to leave during the night, I was prepared.

I slept with one eye open.

andrea

I was so excited that Boss was taking me to Disneyland. It wasn't like I hadn't been there before. I'd been about ten times, but after all it was the *'Happiest Place on Ear*th'. I was excited that I was going with someone that I enjoyed being with. I had the best of both worlds with Boss... she was fun, like a kid, and made me laugh; yet she was responsible and made me feel safe . I knew she would look out for me.

When going to places where there were large crowds I would get very nervous about getting lost. When I had been with Doris and the kids to Disneyland, her daughter never left my side. She liked me and considered me the 'fun adult'. She knew if she stuck with me, she'd get the most out of the day. So I always had her tugging at me saying, wait up; I'm going with you. Then of course, Doris wouldn't let her child out of her sight, in turn, keeping me in sight.

I had insisted that we leave as early in the morning as possible. I knew from past experiences, that the later in the day it got, the louder the Voices would get. I was prone to headaches and seizures during the evening hours. So if we got up there early, I'd have more time to see the sights and ride the rides.

Boss was so good to me that day, as always. She kept up with me as I ran all over trying to squeeze everything in. This trip to Disneyland was the best I'd ever had. There were a few rides that she was too scared to go on, so we did a lot of the kid's rides. But still it was fun.

Everything was going great until we went to watch a 3-D show called, "Honey, I Shrunk the Audience." We put these special glasses on that were given to us as we entered the theater. Suddenly, things started jumping out at us. A cat turned into a roaring lion, mice were running everywhere... It made an impression to say the least. Boss covered up my eyes like I was eight years old and someone had flipped the channel to the Playboy station. I wanted to see what I was missing, but it was too realistic. It stuck with me long after we left the show. For months I was seeing this cat turning into a lion right before my eyes. Even my own cat Gus scared me sometimes, becoming distorted in my perception. After leaving that show, Boss and I decided that we would scratch that attraction permanently off our list.

Finally after hours of running around the park, we both were exhausted and headed over to our hotel room. I was relieved that we decided against staying at my sisters. I had done a pretty good job of hiding my problems from her and my parents. Spending the night might have revealed more about me than I was prepared to expose.

Once we were settled in, I turned on the T.V. and caught my favorite show, 'Chicago Hope'. Since I didn't have a T.V. hook up in the "blue room" at the Leonard's, I'd missed the show since I had moved in. I was anxious to see what I had been missing. Unfortunately, I don't remember the ending of the show.

The next thing I remembered was standing outside a 7-Eleven, and a man coming up to me and giving me a dollar to buy a cup of coffee. I was shivering terribly. He must have seen that I was cold and thought I was homeless.

"Oh crap," I thought to myself. I don't recognize my surroundings and it's cold out. Where is Boss? Where am I? My worst fear had come true. I was lost in Anaheim.

Something inside me told me to "start walking." So I headed down the sidewalk not sure of anything. I'd gone about two blocks when I looked over and saw Boss's car. It was parked in the first stall, at the edge of a parking lot near the sidewalk.

"Well at least I found her car, I thought to myself. "But now what? Do I stay with the car? Do I explore the building next to it?" Again something inside me told me to stay with the car.

As I stood there staring at it, I heard my name and footsteps running up behind me. I turned around and saw Boss. I was relieved and so was she. She put her arms around me and held me so tight I thought I was going to break.

I could tell she was upset. I was too. But I was really glad to be with her again. I didn't understand what was going on, or that I'd wandered off from a hotel room. I just wanted her to take me home.

It wasn't until the next day on the drive home, that Boss explained everything that had happened the night before. I thought this was going to be the last of our 'outings' together.

Wait for the Lord; be strong and take heart and wait for the Lord. Psalm 27:14

Chapter Twenty

The Neurologist

linda

A few days prior to Andrea's appointment with the neurologist, I went into our physician directory to check on the doctor's profile. To my excitement, Dr. Ferrone's bio listed research in brain disorders, specifically in schizophrenia, as his sub-specialty. I was elated.

Finally the day arrived for the visit with the neurologist. Andrea was very nervous and showing it. I felt bad for her, but it would help my case if the doctor could see her in an anxious state. She was sitting on the exam table with her head down covering her face. Her legs were drawn up against her chest and she had her arms wrapped tightly around her legs.

When the doctor walked in, I liked him right away. He was in his early sixties and had a warm smile. After greeting Andrea and me, he sat down and quickly scanned the notes that the nurse had written. I had also sent ahead of time the list of symptoms that I had put together for Dr Easton. I could see he was reading it.

After Dr. Ferrone was done reading he looked up at me curiously and smiled. He looked at Andrea and asked how she was doing. She mumbled something about being nervous, in which he responded tenderly, she need not be. Dr. Ferrone then turned to me and asked why I thought that she was having seizures. I thought it was an odd question for him to ask. Wasn't it obvious from the information in the chart notes? After giving him a brief explanation of what I would witness when Andrea would have these episodes, he said that he would run some tests, but he doubted she was having seizures. I then whispered something about her possibly having schizophrenia. He said she probably should see a psychiatrist for that. I was shocked.

"Didn't you do some extensive studies on schizophrenia and how it relates to the brain?"

Looking at me bewildered, he said, "No, I haven't".

"I read that you have done research relating directly to schizophrenia."

"I am sorry, but I have very little knowledge of psychiatric disorders. Where did you read that I had done research in the area of psychiatry?"

I grabbed my purse and pulled out the printout of his accomplishments off the Internet. He looked and it and smiled. "I have no idea who put this in my Bio".

I was ready to burst into tears. I showed him the disability form as I was struggling not to cry. I explained that I needed this filled out in order to get her some funding.

He looked at me with compassion and said, "I am sorry, I can't fill that out stating she has a seizure disorder without running some tests first". I told him I understood and could he order the tests as soon as possible? He asked me why I haven't taken Andrea to a psychiatrist. I told him that CMS would not cover psychiatric services. That was why I was so excited about him being her patient. I thought we would kill two birds with one stone. Andrea would get someone knowledgeable on seizure disorders and also help with her schizophrenia.

He looked at Andrea and started asking her what I thought were odd questions. "Do you feel like hurting yourself?"

"No".

"Do you feel like killing yourself?"

"No."

"Have you ever thought of killing yourself?"

"Yes."

He looked at me and said, "The County doesn't pay for psychiatric services unless it is considered an emergency. I am sending Andrea down to the emergency room and requesting a psychiatrist see her immediately. In the meantime, I will have my front desk schedule an EEG."

I had figured out what Dr. Ferrone had done. He was looking for an excuse to get her emergency psychiatric care. He knew that County Medical Services would pay for *'emergent'* psychiatric care. I just wanted someone to see her and agree that she had a disability.

By this time, Andrea wasn't doing well, which played in our favor. I felt like I was the only one in the world that could see that she had a problem. Maybe I was the delusional one. As I looked at her sitting there, twenty-seven years old, with a teddy bear held close to her chest and a baby blanket wrapped around her arm, I just wanted to cry. She caught me staring at her and gently smiled at me. I knew Andrea loved me. I loved Andrea and God loved us both.

We had been waiting in the ER for almost an hour when Andrea wanted to go find something to drink. I suggested we go to the café quickly and get a soda. I went to the front desk to inform the receptionist of our plan and to let her know we would be right back. As I was waiting to get her attention, Andrea was reading the log left on the counter. It had names and chief complaints of those waiting to be seen. She looked down the list for her name. She freaked out when she saw what they wrote.

"Boss, I am not suicidal."

"I know sweetheart, but that was the only way we could see a psychiatrist."

"I don't want to see a psychiatrist. I don't want to be locked up."

"You're not. If they want to admit you in the hospital I will say no."

"Boss, they lock people up that are suicidal. I do not want to be locked up."

I finally convinced her. I was relieved that she had come to trust me. Late that afternoon three doctors examined Andrea.

Each physician questioned why Dr. Ferrone sent her down to the ER. I could hear them out in the hallway talking. I sensed that they were a little confused. One of the doctors asked to talk to me privately. I gave a brief explanation of Andrea's problems and explained that during Dr. Ferrone's exam, he felt she was thinking of committing suicide. My words sounded so foolish as they were coming out of my mouth. Andrea looked anything but suicidal that day. She looked more like a child ready to cry and just wanted to be held.

The doctor looked at me and asked what I thought. I never had any problem speaking my mind and now was no exception. I let him have it with both barrels.

"I think she is schizophrenic with a seizure disorder, and if she doesn't get medical care soon, we might lose her. Is it not obvious she has some serious issues? I have seen her psychotic, catatonic and physically ill. She has no income and needs some funding for some basics, like food and shelter. If the State of California can dish out all the money they do for abortions, can they not pay for the obvious care this young woman needs? I need this darn form filled out before I can move forward. As I flashed the form in front of him, he told me he was sorry and understood. I think he was just saying that to avoid a political discussion with an irate woman.

He said he was going to give me prescriptions for her psychosis, which I quickly learned in the game meant, hallucinations, delusions and hearing of voices. He was also going to give her something for her anxiety. The prescriptions would last until Monday. He made me promise that I would stay with her over the next three days (suicide watch), and call County Mental Health first thing Monday morning. He said they would give me more medication without cost.

andrea

Boss was concerned about my seizures. I had gotten used to having them and I didn't know what the big deal was. I had bigger problems. My hallucinations were getting so severe I was barely getting any sleep at night. I'd wake up in the morning, and I would find leaves and twigs in my bed and shoes. I was obviously running from something into the avocado groves. One particular time, when the weather was bad, I must have spent the night in the rain, because in the morning I was soaked and muddy.

I realized that I was doing things at night I couldn't remember. I felt like I was 'Jeckle and Hyde'. I started worrying that I was going to hurt someone. I was also worried I would wander down the mountain, and end up getting in some trucker's truck and wind up in Georgia, or worse, Egypt.

A couple of times I woke up injured. I bumped my head once, and busted my chin open another time. One morning I woke up to find my left arm scraped with what felt like a rug burn. It took at least two months for that to heal, and I still bear the scar. Even in my drinking days, I did not 'wake up' or 'come to' with so many unexplained bumps and bruises.

The nights were getting harder and harder. Back at my old apartment, I had the luxury of drinking when things got bad. The alcohol would help me to get at least a few hours of 'passed out sleep'. But now that I was at the Leonard's, and under Boss's direction and supervision, she didn't want me to drink. Without the alcohol, I was lucky to make it through the night without injury or wandering. Still, I honored Boss's request the best I could.

Boss kept taking me to different doctors, each with the same result. "Nothing is wrong with her," they'd say.

Are they the crazy one's or am I? I knew *something* had to be wrong with me! Well now she was taking me to see a neurologist at the medical center. I wasn't thrilled about it, but Boss kept telling me, "This is good Andie. We need him to fill out the forms I have so you can get some funding and get off that mountain."

That was a language I understood. Getting off that mountain was my biggest, my only priority in life. The days kept getting longer, and the nights kept getting harder. I wanted my *own* place. I was tired of always being under somebody's thumb, under his or her rules. I wanted some real independence for once in my life.

So I took the bus down and met up with Boss to see the neurologist. At least maybe this quack can give me something for my seizures, I thought. Little did I know what I was in store for that day. I went into an appointment at around 11am, and I would not get out of that dreaded hospital until well after dark.

The neurologist came in and he was pleasant looking, and pleasant talking. He had a soothing bedside manner about him. But when I heard Boss tell him about my seizures, it seemed to me that he didn't believe her. He acted as though I wasn't having any problems.

At one point Boss was close to tears. They were talking softly, and I couldn't hear everything they were saying. Then the neurologist turned to me and asked me some bizarre questions. "Have you ever thought of killing yourself?" he asked me.

I thought it was odd of him to ask that. And after I answered "yes", we were suddenly on our way out of there.

"Whew" I thought to myself. That was all I had to say? Just tell him I had been suicidal in the past, and I'm out of there? I was relieved. I was finally out of there and getting out of this place.

But then Boss told me we had to go downstairs to the Emergency Room.

"Why?" I whined.

"This is good," she said again.

"Good for you maybe," I thought. For me this was a nightmare.

I don't remember much of the rest of the day. I soon became very overwhelmed and the Voices took over. I know that a couple different doctors came in and checked me out. And I also remember that I had to take my clothes off and sit there in one of their stupid hospital gowns. I know now that they did that purposely to keep me from running out of the hospital prematurely. Let me tell you though, that it wasn't the gown that kept me there, but Boss. I wanted to please her. I had a lot of love and respect for her, and I wanted her approval of me.

Come to me, all you who are weary and burdened, and I will give you rest. Matt 11:28

Chapter Twenty-One

The Night Life

linda

Once home Andrea was exhausted and needed help getting out of the car and to her room. She was having problems walking. She said her legs did not want to cooperate. Once I got her settled, which simply meant I got her on her bed, I called Tom. I told him about our dreadful day and my promise to supervise Andrea until she could be seen on Monday. I had hoped that Andrea would have been willing to come stay at my apartment, but that was not something she was comfortable doing. I have come to understand that people suffering from any type of mental illness find change very difficult to handle. Andrea needed her own bed in her own room.

After my brief phone call with Tom, I went to check on Andrea. She was sitting in her rocker, with earphones on. It took me a couple of gentle attempts to get her attention. She pulled her earphones off and looked at me bewildered.

"What's wrong?" I asked.

"What are you doing here?"

In the short couple minutes that it took me to make the phone call, Andrea had no recollection of me bringing her home and me telling her that I was going to stay the night.

I hadn't told her that the ER physician released her in my care providing I keep an eye on her. I was afraid her paranoia would run wild. She must have asked me at least thirty times today if she was going to be committed.

Whenever I would ask Andrea how she slept the night before, she would reply, "Don't ask". I knew that sleep didn't come easy for her, but I had no idea the activities that went on in her room during the night. Even as I attempt to explain it to you now, I find it hard to believe what I witnessed that night and many times after that.

Andrea finally went to bed around midnight after rocking in her chair with her earphones on for over an hour. Fully dressed with shoes on she ran and jumped on the bed. It was as if she had to get in bed before something got her. It wasn't long until I was awaken by the sound of her jumping out of bed and running to the bathroom. I looked at my watch and only an hour had gone by. I waited for her to come out of the bathroom from what I considered a reasonable amount of time. The bathroom light was off. I got up and went to the bathroom door and called her name. She did not answer. I opened the door slowly and turned on the light.

"Ah-h-h-h-h," she screamed.

To my surprise, Andrea was cowering in the corner, with her eyes covered as if she was expecting something to grab her.

"What's wrong honey?"

"Ah-h-h-h-h," she said as she covered her eyes and curled up tighter in a ball.

"Andrea, please, it's me, why are you frightened?"

The closer I got to her the more she would cower. She obviously was experiencing something that scared her. I wondered if she was sleepwalking. It took me at least ten minutes to get her off the floor and back into bed. The whole time she kept scanning the room as if she had to prepare herself just in case she was attacked. Even as she laid in bed she couldn't stay still. I recalled the night at Ralph's market and saw a resemblance to her behavior.

After about twenty minutes she became very quiet. She would not allow me to leave the light on in the hallway or bathroom, so it was hard for me to observe her. I touched her hand and could feel her fingers clenched. I then touched her face gently. I could tell that her teeth were clinched and her neck was stiff. Andrea was having a seizure. Every thing seemed so bizarre and wrong. Nothing seemed to fit or make sense. I slowly put my knees on the ground, and placed my head and hands on her bed and began to pray.

"Lord, I don't know what I am doing. I don't understand what is wrong with Andrea and I am scared, not to mention tired and frustrated. I know Lord that Andrea's and my path have crossed for a reason. I know you have only asked that I love her, and you would do the rest, but Lord I am not sure at this point if I can do this. I feel as if I am in the middle of the ocean with her and that we are both drowning. I feel so alone. My family is trying to understand and be supportive, but miss me. My friends are concerned that my involvement with Andrea is affecting my relationship with others. My co-workers think I am the one that is nuts and should see a shrink. God, what are you thinking? Why me? Please guide me Lord. I'm lost."

As I knelt quietly, hoping that Jesus would walk in the door and relieve me of my duties, I suddenly felt a peace come over me. Sing. What? Sing. God are you asking me to sing? Ok, I'll sing. I climbed onto the bed and laid beside Andrea. Quietly I started singing. An old familiar hymn came to mind that I hadn't sung in years....'Jesus.... Jesus.....Jesus.....there is something about that name...Master, Savior, Jesus.....like the fragrance after the rain....

Within a few minutes I could feel her body become limber and start to move. She eventually turned her face towards me and smiled. I could see blood where she had bitten her lip during the seizure. She rolled over and went back to sleep.

Sleep was not a friend of hers. Before an hour had gone by, she was awake again screaming that "they" had scissors and were stabbing at her eyes. She jumped up again and was back in the corner of the bathroom on the floor, frightened and unable to move due to fear. The whole situation played itself out again, including me singing her back to sleep.

If Andrea got a total of three hours sleep that night I would have been surprised. She was up and down all night long. The next morning when I tried to talk to her about it, all she said was that she never slept very well at night. To me that was an understatement. She obviously did not have the same recollection I had of the night.

Cast all your cares on the Lord and He will sustain you; He will never let you down. Psalms 55:22

Chapter Twenty-Two

The Redecorating

andrea

One morning I woke up to find I had done some redecorating. Upon opening my eyes, I immediately reached for my glasses, but they weren't where I always put them. Sitting up in bed, I instinctively looked around my room. Although everything was blurry I could see that some things were different.

First of all, Pamela's 10 inch T.V. was missing, as was her clock radio. Second, my T.V. was shoved oddly against the wall. Also there was a distinct smell. Vomit. It was matted in my hair. Noticing some other things that weren't right in my room, and not being able to locate my glasses, I was almost in tears. I knew something had happened the night before, but what?

Immediately I grabbed my phone and called Boss. I was so distraught, I was hoping that talking to her would make everything back the way it was.

"Oh Boss... Oh Boss...," I said walking around with my phone, "I really did it this time."

"What's the matter?"

"Oh Boss... I don't know what I did last night. I smell like puked salmon and I can't find my glasses," I said fighting back the tears. "Oh Boss…, I really did it this time. I am in so much trouble. Arn is going to really be pissed."

"It's okay Andie," Boss said trying to reassure me.

Finally I found my glasses bent out of shape, on the floor behind my T.V. Putting them on, I could see clearly now. "Oh Boss… Oh Boss…," I moaned surveying the damage.

When I walked into the bathroom, it got even worse. Water from the cat's bowl was all over the floor; my cat's food and water bowl were upside down in his litter box. My Legos were all over the counter, in the sink, and even in Gus's litter box. My latest Lego creation, which took me hours to complete, was destroyed. Soap, lotions, all the items that were suppose to be on the sink top were scattered everywhere. I saw where I had vomited on the floor. Then something caught my eye. There was a hole in the wall! Still walking around with the mobile phone in my hand, I was speechless. I could hear Boss asking, "What honey…what?

"Oh Boss, it's bad. It's really bad."

"What?"

I couldn't answer her. I was mortified.

"What!" I heard Boss scream through the phone.

"Oh Boss, there's a hole in the wall. I put a hole in the wall. Oh Boss…!"

I stood there staring at the wall, shocked at what I had done. I was desperate to remember. But I couldn't.

Even though Boss was on the phone with me, I suddenly felt very alone. I felt like I didn't even know myself. I was ashamed and frustrated at what I had done. Finally the tears started flowing. I couldn't hold it in any longer. What was wrong with me? Why couldn't I remember what had happened? Did the Leonard's know about this? How was I going to face them? If they didn't know, how was I going to break it to them? One thing I knew for sure. I was in trouble. Big trouble.

Later Lin told me that she heard this banging noise in perfect rhythm and it woke her up. She thought to herself, "Oh my gosh, my parents must be having sex!" Afraid to get up and investigate any further, she stayed in bed.

Arnold told me that he heard the noise and thought it was coming from outside. Getting up to check it out, he realized it was coming from downstairs. Coming down, he found me in the bathroom, hitting the wall with a coffee mug. He said he tried to get me to stop, but I had already made a nice sized hole in the wall. Once he got the mug away from me, he said I collapsed onto the floor and started vomiting. He tried to keep me from laying in it, but I was oblivious. He said I kept asking for Pamela, but he told me that she was asleep. Eventually he got me into bed satisfied that I was done redecorating for the night and ready to call it a night.

Pamela had a story herself. Earlier in the evening, before Arnold had come down, she had heard a crash from downstairs, and came to see what happened. She found me trying to keep my balance, wedging myself between the bed and the dresser. She helped me into my rocking chair, and then removed her T.V. and radio from my room to keep them safe.

After hearing about what had happened, I struggled to keep my dignity. I knew that I lost time and got confused, but the Leonard's witnessing my behavior was difficult to deal with.

Of course, everyone had his or her own theory on *why* I had done what I did. Arnold thought I was just lonely downstairs and wanted some attention. Lin wanted to know what I was drinking. Pamela was reserved and kept quiet as to not embarrass me. And Boss told me I had probably started hallucinating, and I was trying to kill what ever it was that I saw on the wall.

With all their opinions, I had my own. I was just plain nuts.

linda

It wasn't long after Andrea and I hung up the phone that I received a detailed e-mail from Arnold explaining the events of the night before.

Eventually Arnold repaired the damages, but it remained a reminder for all to see for over six weeks. Above the holes Arn had written in black marker....

"ANDREA WAS HERE!"

Look at what the Lord has done for you....do not fear or be discouraged. Deuteronomy 1:21

Chapter Twenty-Three

The Psychiatrist

linda

Since I wasn't getting anywhere with the CMS primary physician nor the neurologist in getting the disability formed signed, it was suggested that I take Andrea to a psychiatrist. I knew that her mom had a good relationship with one she had seen, so I gave her mom a call. Apparently Dr. Connors already had some history with Andrea. Marilee had taken Andrea to see him once when Andrea was a teenager. He also knew about Andrea through discussions that her mom had with him. Andrea's parents had taken her to a number of psychologists during her childhood, but Andrea hated going and nothing seemed to get resolved. Her family knew that Andrea had some emotional problems, but not to the magnitude that they turned out to be.

I called the psychiatrist office and they gave me an appointment the very next day.

Dr. Connors was a small, quiet mannered man. I found him very pleasant and reassuring. Andrea was her natural, nervous wreck going into his office. It was a fairly large office with windows across the back, overlooking a garden. The room had a dark cherry wood desk in the corner. Dr. Connors had his chair face outward toward us, with his back to his desk.. We sat in two nice size chairs facing him with our back to the large picture window. I was a little disappointed that there was no couch. I had never been in a psychiatrist office before, but I had seen enough movies to know that there should have been a couch. Of course, I was the only one of the two of us that was relaxed enough to lounge.

The same list of symptoms that I had given Dr. Easton and Dr. Ferrone had been faxed to Dr. Connors a few days before our scheduled appointment. After the first session, in which he asked Andrea a number of questions, he filled out the disability form without hesitation or reservation. The diagnosis listed was Chronic Paranoid Schizophrenic with long-term disability not limited to twelve months. Talk about a bittersweet emotion. I was elated that I finally I got a physician to sign the tattered disability form, that I had been carrying around for months. However seeing the diagnosis in writing, confirmed by a physician, felt like someone had kicked me in the stomach. Andrea only looked at me scared.

Dr. Connors saw Andrea one more time before telling us that if Andrea insisted on staying on the drops and not go on medication, he would not nor could manage her care. He felt that unless Andrea went on medication, it would be impossible for him to help her.

I was torn. Dr. Easton was confident that once Andrea's system balanced out, the symptoms would disappear. He claimed success with many others with mental illnesses. He also warned us that the medication was a drug and would act as a poison in her system. I kept asking Andrea what she wanted and she would always insist that she wanted to give the drops more time. She did not like the idea of taking medication. She was paranoid of all the side effects. Other than still having symptoms, Andrea looked well and healthy. We both thought the drops had promise and wanted to stick with the original plan.

andrea

Boss had been dragging me all over town trying to get someone to fill out this form that she had. Soon she realized I would have to see a psychiatrist. My mom had seen one, and I had even seen him once before in an effort by my parents to help me with my problems. I saw Dr. Connors during my high school years.

Boss got an appointment scheduled, and we went to see him. I recognized him immediately, yet I was as wound up as I'd ever been in anticipation of seeing a psychiatrist. Something about him being a 'shrink' scared me. I knew he was interpreting every move I made, and analyzing every statement I said.

Once in his office the Voices became very loud, but it was the demons up in the corners that were really bothering me. I was so afraid, I wanted to run out of his office and never look back. Boss had been drilling me not to be a 'turtle', and to be honest with him, but I was so afraid if he found out about the demons and the Voices, I would be committed faster than they could forge my signature.

Boss seemed delighted. I had never known anyone to put so much effort in to getting me well as she had demonstrated. I remember Dr. Connors being especially calm. How could he be so calm with all these demons hanging out in his office? That worried me that maybe he was in control of the demons. Maybe they listened to him and followed his orders. Suddenly it wasn't a maybe, I was convinced. He would know if I was lying to him, and then he would unleash the demons on me.

So when he asked me a few questions, I was very careful with the answers I gave. At one point he told me I seemed a little preoccupied. "What is he trying to do?" I thought. "Trick me?"

Keeping my answers as simple as possible, I responded, "Yes, I am." I was not going to give this warlord any more information than needed.

Finally we were out of there. Boss got the form signed, and I left Dr. Connors in there alone with his demons. I was glad to be free again. I was relieved until I read what he'd written on the form. "Chronic Paranoid Schizophrenic." I didn't like the chronic part, and I didn't like the paranoid part, nor the schizophrenic part either. I searched Boss's face for reassurance. I was internally begging her to tell me, "Don't worry sweetheart, It's not true."

I could see the compassion and love in her eyes, but the reassuring words never came.

Praise be to the God and Father of our Lord Jesus Christ, the Father of compassion and the God of all comfort, who comforts us in all our troubles, so that we can comfort those in any trouble with the comfort we ourselves have received from God. 2 Corinthians 1:3

Chapter Twenty-Four

The Blood

linda

Andrea called me this morning, chipper as usual. Arn had an errand to do in town and agreed to drop her off at the transit center. Andrea's trips would take over two hours that entailed two bus transfers. She would call me periodically during her trip to tell me where she was, and anything exciting that might have happened during her travels. Since getting confused was not uncommon for her, I welcome the updates. This particular day around 1:30 I realized that I had not heard from Andrea. It seemed odd, but I didn't give it too much thought. It could be a good sign. She was probably having a good day and didn't feel the need to check in. It was usually when she wasn't feeling right and getting paranoid, that she would find the need to call often.

When 2:30 came around and I hadn't heard from her, I was concerned. It really was unlike her. When 3:00 came and went, I was seriously worried. She was supposed to arrive on the 3:00 bus. Around 3:30 I got a call from an automated computer asking if I would accept a collect call from, (I heard a frightened voice say), Andrea. By the sound in her voice, I could tell something was wrong. I could not hit the #1 button fast enough to indicate "yes" I'll take the call. Just at that moment, I heard the clink of the phone. "I'm sorry the caller has hung up," said the computerized voice. I was beside myself. I knew she was in trouble and trying to contact me. I called the Leonards to see if they had heard from her, but their line was busy.

As soon as I got home, I called the Leonards again. I was praying that they would reassure me that she was home and safely in her room. Instead there was no answer. There was no bus route to their area, so she would have had to call them to come pick her up. There was no answer. I told myself that she probably got confused and lost and called them to come get her, and that was why they were not home.

It was around 8:45 p.m. and I was cleaning up the kitchen when our apartment monitor rang indicating we had a visitor. The caller was a man who did not identify himself. All he said was that we had a visitor who needed assistance and someone better come down. Tom said the man sounded very concerned. I immediately knew that our visitor was Andrea.

"Honey, I am sure it's Andie. I'll go down."

I literally ran down the stairs not wanting to wait for the elevator. At first, I could not see her. It was dark and there was no one standing by the gate under the light. The man who called must have left. As I flung open the gate I saw something move in the corner. I could see a body cowering.

"Andie is that you?"

As I went over to her, I was not prepared for what I saw. She had blood smeared everywhere. I could see that the blood was dry. She had it on the side of her face, in her hair, on her hands, on the right side of her leg, and all over her white sweatshirt.

"Sweetheart, what in the world happened to you?" I could see in her eyes that she was scared. She did not say a word. I put my arm around her and the two of us went up to my apartment.

Tom had gone back to his study and was working at his computer when we walked in. I took her straight to the bathroom knowing that I needed to clean her up to determine where the blood had come from. She was very quiet and not responsive to any of my questions. I took her sweatshirt off and put it, along with her socks in the bathtub to soak. Tom heard me talking to her and came over to the bathroom door.

"She's ok, I just need to clean her up."

I gave Tom a look that told him to leave. The last thing I needed was a squeamish man looking over my shoulders doing nothing. With a warm washcloth, I started at the top. I was slowly cleaning the blood off as I looked for a puncture or cut. I saw nothing. I continued to ask her. "Andie, what happen, where did this blood come from? Where are you hurt?" She would just look at me as if she was waiting for me to explain what had happened to her.

I finally found where the blood had come from. As I was working the washcloth down her right leg I stimulated the wounds. They started to bleed again. To my horror she had about fifty small puncture wounds down the outside of her leg. It looked as if someone had attacked her with a fork!

I had no sooner finished cleaning her up when she jumped back, looked at the ground, screamed and jumped up on the counter. Andrea yelled the word "snakes". Andrea was obviously hallucinating. She was seeing snakes on my floor and was trying to get her feet off the ground. She tried to get me to do the same. Tom came running into the bathroom.

"Honey, she is hallucinating, please pray!"

"Andie, it's Tom, it's ok, let's go into the living room. Linda and I will pray for God's protection, and peace on the three of us."

Once I told Tom that trying to tell a person who is hallucinating that what they see is not real, doesn't work. You can't reason with a psychotic person. I was impressed that he remembered. Instead of telling her that there were no snakes on the bathroom floor, he tapped into what would calm her without validating her reality.

The three of us sat on the living room floor and Tom started to pray. I had Andrea in my arms and I could feel her trembling. Tom got up after his prayer and said he was going to put on some music. He put on America Worships, White As Snow CD. The soft music was peaceful and the words were soothing and encouraging. Things seem to be calming down. Tom felt comfortable leaving us alone to go back to his studies. As I softly sang along with the songs, I could feel her body relax. She eventually fell asleep in my arms. I had propped myself up against the couch, so I was comfortable. I held her in my arms on the floor of my apartment that night for over an hour and a half. To this day, Andrea keeps that CD with her at all times. It's what she listens to when life starts to get overwhelming for her.

During the ride back home Andrea remained very quiet. I thought it was best to leave her alone and let her deal with her thoughts. After about twenty minutes she asked if we could stop off at Taco Bell. She said she was hungry. I found that a good sign.

"Andrea, you do realize that the wounds on your leg were inflicted by you."

She very sheepishly said yes.

It was a very sobering evening. I had never discussed Andrea's scars on her legs and arms. Up to this point, I never felt she was ready, but now I thought she was.

"Andrea, do you realize that the same way you were hallucinating and put all those holes in your leg tonight, is the reason you have so many scars on your body?"

"Maybe. I don't want to talk about it."

"I think it would do you good to talk about it. Maybe now is not a good time, but soon."

The following day I called Dr. Connors and made an appointment. Although I believed in the drops, I also believed that we did not have the time to wait for her body to cleanse itself and the healing process to begin. Dr. Connors was relieved that we both came to our senses and wrote up a prescription for one of the newer psychotic medications on the market. On May 7, 1999 Andrea started taking an anti-psychotic medication.

andrea

One afternoon, a few days before Mother's Day, Arn dropped me in town to catch the bus. I was going into San Diego to meet Boss. I decided that on my way down, I would stop off at the bank. I had received a small tax refund check which I had deposited the previous week. My plan was to get some money out of my account to buy two Mother's Day cards; and went to the bank I'd used while working for UPS. It was a small bank inside a grocery store, and had three teller windows. In the past, I would just walk in and talk to the familiar teller, and complete my transactions without an ID or ATM card. Since they knew me, and I knew my account number, I was usually done within a couple of minutes.

Today was different. As I approached the teller window I searched for a familiar face and could not find one. Boss had me recently close my old account and open up a new one. Boss was concerned because I had given my security number for my ATM card to my roommate in the past. She said that once I got on disability, the money would be directly deposited and she felt more secure knowing that I was the only one that could access the account. I just thought Boss was being paranoid, but I went along with it anyway.

I walked up to the teller, and said, "I want twenty dollars please."

"Okay Mam, what is your account number?"

"I don't know," I said. "I just want twenty dollars."

"Do you have an account with us?" she asked me.

"Yes of course. I just want twenty dollars please," I said getting a little irritated.

"What is your account number?" she asked again.

Again I responded, "I don't know. I just want twenty dollars."

We went back and forth a couple more times, and by this time I was becoming anxious and overwhelmed, and the teller was becoming suspicious of me.

I couldn't understand why she wouldn't just give me twenty dollars and send me on my way. I had done this a hundred times before.

Then she asked to see some ID, to which I responded that I didn't have any. I didn't understand why she was making this so difficult. They had my money, and I just wanted twenty dollars of it.

Now the woman was totally irritated with me, and called for her supervisor to come over.

I was having trouble hearing her; the Voices were so loud. I couldn't hear a thing she was saying. Completely frustrated and overwhelmed by it all, I turned and ran out of the store. I was fighting back the tears, and dealing with paranoid thoughts of the bank manager coming after me with a gun. I also had visions of the customers looking at me like I was insane. I couldn't take it anymore; I had to run as fast as I could.

I needed to call Boss. I just wanted to hear her voice. I knew she would reassure me that everything was going to be okay.

I went to the nearest pay phone, and dialed 1 (800) Collect. After listening to the instructions, I punched in Boss's work number. I turned and could see the demons gaining ground so I had to drop the phone receiver and started running.

Turning around to watch my back, I saw the demons coming after me. They were huge and their teeth were big and sharp and bloody, and they were closing in on me.

A while later I found another pay phone and attempted again to call Boss. I so desperately wanted to hear her voice. I got as far as saying my name when I could see the demons from the corner of my eye. Hanging up the phone, I ran. I ran as fast as I could. I had my big backpack with me, and wasn't having much success in getting away from the demons. I ran through the parking lot, dodging cars and people. I had to get away from the demons. They were coming after me.

I could hear and feel their breath on my neck. I knew any moment they would have me. And that's when I blacked out.

I would be missing in action for the next ten hours. All I remember of that day was I was doing a lot of running. Every time I would try to stop and call Boss, the demons would start to catch up. Somehow I managed to get to downtown San Diego.

It was very dark and cold when I finally found Boss's apartment. It was a gated community, and so I had to wait outside for someone to come and open the gate for me to be able to get inside. However, when someone would come to the gate, they saw me and quickly slammed it shut. Finally one young man came to the gate, and saw me. He asked me if I was okay, and I told her I was trying to find Boss.

He looked at me oddly, and then asked me if Boss had a last name.

I must have remembered "Edmunds" because a minute later he was on the speaker talking to Tom.

Soon I heard someone running down the stairs, and the gate flying open. Standing in front of me was Boss. Why was she looking at me that way? Her face scared me. Was she mad? She then reached down and gently helped me to my feet. She took another look at me and then pulled me close to her and held me real tight. I was relieved. This is where I needed to be.

She looked at me for answers, but I had none to give her. I had no idea what had happened that day. I wasn't concerned about the blood, as much as I was about finally finding her. Both my legs could have been broken at that point and I probably wouldn't have even known. I wasn't in any pain, and the only reason I knew I was bleeding was because I could smell the blood on me.

She took me up to her apartment, and got me cleaned up, all the while asking me what had happened. I was embarrassed that I didn't know. She was so wise. I was hoping she would give them to me.

The rest of the night I was confused, and I don't remember much of it. I do remember Tom praying and Boss holding me and singing softly.

In the days following the incident, I was more scared than I had ever been. I was realizing that I had somehow done this to myself. I had no one to blame for it but me. I was embarrassed. Arnold kept asking me to see my leg, but I wore jeans or covered it up with Band-Aids. It was a tough lesson of reality for me. Maybe, just maybe, the other scars my body bore were *also* self-inflicted. If that was so, I had a lot more wrong with me than I ever thought.

Look at the birds of the air; they do not sow or reap or store away in barns, and yet your heavenly Father feeds them. Are you not much more valuable than they? Matthew 6:26

Chapter Twenty-Five

The Outward Bound Experience

andrea

Boss kept telling me that healing had to be done as a whole. She said I not only needed physical healing, but emotional and spiritual healing. I was now on medication, at least for the time being, and eating healthier than I ever had in my life. My spiritual life had taken a turn for the better. I was praying and reading my Bible everyday, and truly feeling God's working in my life. The emotional healing was going to be the challenge. Boss insisted that I keep communication open with my family and allow them to help me. Forgiveness was something that needed to be done on both sides. My high school years were very hard on my parents and I in turn always thought my parents were hard on me. I had very few memories of when I really made them proud. Sure, I had my music, but I just considered that a God-given talent that didn't really have to do with anything I did. However, my three weeks with the Outward Bound team was different. That was a time I knew for sure that my parents were proud.

Since I was having so much trouble in school, my parents tried different solutions. I went to see counselors, psychologists, psychiatrists, yet nothing seem to help. So as a last ditch effort my parents decided to try one more thing.... Outward Bound.

My parents heard about a highly successful program designed in helping troubled kids. The program was a wilderness experience teaching survival skills. My parents knew that I loved camping and being outdoors. They also knew I was troubled, so they decided to look into it.

It was probably the best thing they ever did for me. Outward Bound was a life-changing experience. It wasn't a cure for the Voices or demons, but it sure helped my self-esteem, which in turn helped me cope with my symptoms.

Outward Bound excursions were available to adults of all ages, in various different elements. There was river rafting, rock climbing, backpacking, and bike riding to name a few. They all varied from three days, to three weeks in the wilderness. I was going to go on a program called 'Youth at Risk' for teens ages 14-17. It was to be in August of 1989, for 24 days. The cost: $2400 - one hundred dollars a day. And that wasn't including the special boots and clothes I would have to buy for the trip.

This wasn't just a 'camping' trip. This was an intense backpacking trip that would include over 100 hiked miles, rock climbing, repelling, and climbing the peak of Black Mountain, about 12,000 feet high. I was excited. I wanted to do it, and was thrilled when my spot was reserved.

My parents took me to REI, a specialized wilderness store, to get my required boots and clothes. I needed a lot of stuff, which added up quickly. By the time we left the store, my parent had forked out over $500. Another unexpected expense was my sunglasses. I needed prescription lenses.

I know my parents were really praying that this trip would change my life. Not just because of the money invested, but because they didn't know where else to turn.

As August got closer, I got more excited. It was very hot in San Diego, but I'd had to buy specially treated long underwear, and wool pants, waterproof jacket, gloves and cap. I wondered how cold it was going to be up there, having to have such warm clothes.

Since Lin knew it was getting closer to the day I would leave for Outward Bound, and we were both a little anxious about not being able to talk on the phone everyday, she thought of a plan. She did one of the sweetest things ever. She went and got some curling ribbon from upstairs, and brought it outside. Then she cut off a little piece and tied it around my middle finger.

"Now when you're out in the middle of nowhere, and you can't get to a phone, you just look at this ribbon and it will remind you that you have a friend here at home that loves you very much," she said. I wore that ribbon all the way through Outward Bound.

Finally the day arrived. With anticipation and excitement I packed my stuff in the family car, a 1984 Volvo. I was on my way, with my parents, to the Sierra Mountains. Since the trip was a twelve-hour venture, my Dad decided to split the driving time in half by stopping off for the night, and continuing the trip the next day.

When we got to our motel, and I was faced with spending a night out of my own bed, I became very anxious. Reality sunk in that it would be almost four weeks before I would sleep in my own bed again. I had Pickles, my teddy bear with me, but even he couldn't comfort me the way I needed. My mind started racing. What if I started hallucinating, and freaking out with my parents in the same room. What if I started hallucinating at night around the other kids? What would the other kids think of me? I really wanted to go home. I wanted the comfort of my own bed, in my own room where my demons could be hidden from the rest of the world. I didn't sleep well that night.

The next morning, my parents noticed the change in me. Sensing my hesitation they tried to encourage me. "You'll have a lot of fun" they said. "You'll make new friends." But everything they said, went in one ear and out the other. I didn't think I'd have fun, and I didn't think I'd make any friends. They would all think I was 'crazy' like the kids at school. But it didn't matter what I thought, because a few hours later, I was at base camp 1, showing my boots to one of the instructors, and then whisked into a large group of kids.

Once we were grouped together, they made us sit down in a big circle on a large patch of grass. Then they went around the circle, making just one request of each of us. What was it? We had to promise not to smoke the entire time, and those that had cigarettes with them, they were to put them in a pile in the center of the circle, and were told we'd get them back when we returned. Fortunately, I was not one of the smokers. I had tried it in the past with my friends, but I wasn't hooked like some of the others.

After that, we were all told to grab our stuff, and we were herded into busses to be bussed to Base Camp 2. Before boarding my mom took a picture and hugged me and told me when it was over, I wouldn't want to come home, and my Dad... well he prayed once more I'm sure, that this trip would make a difference.

The bus ride took about an hour, and the girl sitting next to me became very friendly. I'd assume she was thinking that she'd better make friends with somebody now, because it was going to be a long 24 days. I on the other hand, was a little less inclined to be sociable. I was too busy listening to the Voices and trying to figure out how I was going to survive the next few weeks.

Once we arrived, we were separated into smaller groups of ten, and given three instructors. In our group there were six guys and four girls and our official title was PASD-056. The girl who had befriended me on the bus was put in a different group than mine. So much for her planning ahead.

I immediately liked my instructors, especially the two women, Laurie and Madeline. Marvin was okay, but he was very quiet and the way he looked at me made me a little nervous. I started struggling with the idea that he could read my mind. To get my thoughts off of that, I focused on the others around me.

Each group was given supplies and food rations. The supplies consisted of a pot, a small single burner stove and fuel,

On the Road to Peace

two tarps in case of rain, a couple rolls of T.P., a shovel and a rusty coffee can to burn the used T.P. in. The food was all packaged and almost all of it was 'just add water'. Then there was a first aid kit and some benadine to add to stream water to make it drinkable. All these supplies and rations were split up between each of us.

Individual supplies were given out to each of us also. We were given a sleeping bag, a plastic mug and spoon for eating with the next few weeks, a few yards of webbing to make a climbing harness out of, and a helmet for climbing. As far as personal food went, we each got a bag of trail mix with some much treasured fake M&M's, and a bag of biscuit crackers called 'Bickies'. The first few crackers we forced down were pretty disgusting. But a week or so into the trip, and they were equal to cookies.

After we were given all our personal gear and split up the group gear, we were told to pack our backpacks. I looked around at all the stuff I had that I was supposed to fit in the pack, and I knew this was going to be about an 80lb pack on my back. The others also would be hefty.

The instructors came around and gave us directions on how to pack, and a lot had to re-pack five or six times before they got it all in. Since my Dad had done some backpacking himself, I'd picked up a few tips, so my pack was loaded up pretty quick.

Now that it was packed, I had to try and put it on. But picking up a pack of 80lbs of dead weight wasn't easy. I thought about leaning it against a tree, and then sitting down and strapping myself into it, then grabbing a helpful hand to pull me up. But I was a tough kid inside, and more interested in protecting my pride than protecting my back. So I free-stood it and struggled a bit and 'whola', I got it on. I stood there proud as a peacock, fighting to keep my balance, as I strapped it around my waist and cinched it up tight to take the pressure off my shoulders and back. With a big smile on my face, I was ready to go.

I turned around and noticed some of the guys in my group staring at me. If a girl like me could do it, they were determined to do it as well. But without the previous experience I had hiking with my Dad, they weren't as successful. I noticed most of them had to use the tree and buddy plan. That boosted my self-esteem, and I silently thanked my Dad for the training he'd given me.

Once we all had on our packs, and our instructors got us together, we were off. We had a short but steep hike to make to get to our first official camp on Outward Bound.

As we all started out at a pace set by Marvin, I noticed the guys fulfilling their need to be macho pushed by us girls and took off pretty fast. I watched their steps and I knew they had set too fast of a pace, and they'd run out of steam way before hitting the top. The girls were going slow and keeping up with my pace. Marvin decided he'd go on ahead with the guys, and Laurie and Madeline stayed back with us.

Once I started to warm up, I decided to slowly pick up the pace I had set.

I felt good and was adjusting to the weight of the pack better than I'd expected. So it wasn't long before the conversations of the girls were out of ear shot for me. In about another half-mile, I heard someone coming up behind me. I turned to see Laurie, the instructor.

"You got away from us pretty fast back there. You doing okay?" she asked, obviously concerned I wasn't going to adjust to the weight of my pack and the altitude at the pace I'd set.

"I'm doing fine," I said. "How far do you think we are from camp?"

"Just a couple more miles. But it gains a lot of altitude," she warned me.

I thanked her and kept on steady with my pace. I usually do a lot of counting when I'm climbing steps. So I was counting in sets of four and the Voices were counting and chanting along with me. It was one of those rare moments where the Voices were actually helpful and a pleasant distraction from the physical exertion making me tired.

It was about a mile later, and I was still steady as could be. In fact I was just barely breaking a sweat and my breathing was normal. I turned a corner on the path, and I saw the guys who had taken off so quickly leaning back against some large rocks, panting heavily.

I glanced at each of them and couldn't help but run my mouth off. I didn't want to be cruel; I was just trying to state some facts.

"Big tough guys and you had to stop to take a break?" I teased laughing a little.

I expected to get some snide remark in return, but instead they were all speechless.

I just kept hiking, knowing that if they passed me up, it would have to be while I was still hiking. I knew there was no chance of a minute break for me now.

I kept to my pace, and actually was the first kid to reach the top. Marvin was up there waiting for us, and I could tell he was surprised that I was the first one he saw. He became even more impressed as more and more time passed before the rest of the group showed up.

Even though we were at the top of the mountain, there was still a mile or so to go where we'd camp for the night. The instructors had topographical maps, and looked for flat white or brown clearings. White clearings meant rock slabs to set up on, and brown meant large dirt areas. Green clearings on the map were meadows, and you can't camp in a meadow because you'll kill the grass by trampling on it. So for the next 23 nights, we slept on dirt and leaves and pine needles if we were lucky, and hard rock slabs if we weren't.

That first night, they brought out the two tarps, and taught us how to secure them to trees to make shelter. While we were doing that, Marvin started working on making dinner for us. It wasn't much. Almost everything we would eat was flavored powder that you just added water to. The joke about our diet was that everything we ate was just add water, even if you wanted water… just add water.

After eating dinner, we sat in a circle and introduced ourselves more and talked a little bit about why we were here, and what our interests were on the outside. It was all a lot of small talk, and I don't think any of us knew the bond that would develop between us all.

That night when it was time to go to bed and get some sleep, it was hard for me. The girl next to me was sniffling, and asked me if I missed my parents. I answered her that I missed a lot of stuff, but definitely not my parents. I was glad to be away from them. Not that I didn't love my parents, it was just a normal teenage reaction to my parents trying to send me to every counselor who would listen, trying to 'fix' me. It all scared me. I was afraid one of these shrinks would find out about the Voices and the demons and I'd be committed to a hospital for the rest of my life. So no, I did not miss all the drama I attributed to my parents that I left behind in San Diego.

Soon though, I felt myself close to tears. This was going to be hard. I was stuck out in the middle of nowhere, with a bunch of people I'd just met a few hours ago. I missed my bed, and I *really* missed Pickles. My teddy bear had been a part of me since I was three months old. I never went to bed without him. I missed Lin and the Leonard's, and now, I was even starting to miss my family. I fingered the ribbon Lin had tied around my finger. At least I had a little bit of home with me.

On the third day, we started having fun. We stopped at a rock formation and were taught the first basics of rock climbing and repelling. I was a little nervous, and the Voices were telling me I was going to fall to my death. But still, I fought through them, and focused on this new exhilarating sport. I saw this as a once in a lifetime opportunity and I started having a blast.

Even though it was the middle of August, one afternoon it started raining, and it rained hard. When we got into camp that night we were soaked. Cooking was almost impossible and we had to wait a long time to eat. Then suddenly the storm turned electrical. It was not only pouring now, but also thundering and lightening as well.

I really got scared because the lightening seemed so close. The instructors too became concerned and told us to find a large tree and stand one foot from the trunk. I had no choice at that moment but to go to the Maker of the elements. I prayed for safety for all of us. God seemed to hear, because about thirty minutes later, the lightening stopped and the rain let up. The next morning when we woke up, it was a clear sunny day.

On the tenth day of OB, we hiked into our second base camp, and met up with all the other students on the expedition. Food and fuel supplies were brought in by horse back. This was probably my least favorite day of OB. I liked being in my small group, and felt overwhelmed by so many people. I noticed that my friends had no problem socializing with the others, swapping stories, bragging about our climbs. To me it just meant criticism by others, even though I wasn't getting any. I was paranoid that everyone was talking about me, telling those in PASD-056 lies about me. When we headed back out that afternoon, it took me until the next day to feel comfortable with my group again.

This was the second portion of our expedition, and the instructors started expecting more out of us. Each day, we were taught a new skill needed to survive in the wilderness. Very rarely did we hike on trails, and we each had to learn how to use the topographical map and compass to navigate our way through the mountains. Also we learned how to light the stove and cook for the group. We already knew how to pack our packs now, and how to evenly distribute the supplies, but the navigating was more difficult to learn.

One day the instructors told us we were going to have a big hiking day. That worried all of us, because we had been hiking 12 to sometimes even 15 miles over rough terrain of brush and rocks a day. What could be harder than that?

Well this day we were going to hike to the top of Black Mountain, a summit of a mere 12,000 feet. Still, it kicked our butts. Once we hit about 11,000 the altitude started to set in. Breathing became a little more difficult, and our bodies started to feel the strain.

Hiking it wasn't all too easy either. After 10,000 feet, we were climbing over large black rocks that were very sharp and hot from the sun. A few hundred feet from the top, we hit a section where we had to secure a couple rope lines and tether ourselves in just to climb parallel across the rocks over a *very* steep section. If we were to fall, without being tied in, we would have fallen to our death. I felt the risk exhilarating. It was a little unnerving to all of us, but a couple of the girls really got scared and didn't want to continue on.

Wanting to quit though was never an option on OB. We just had to keep pressing on, no matter what the challenge.

Still, it took the girls a little longer than the rest of us, and we had nothing to do but sit in the blazing sun and one hundred-degree weather. Finally, when we had all crossed, we could move on together as a group.

When we reached the top though, the view was spectacular. Almost every day, I'd been taking pictures of what I thought were 'once in a lifetime views' and tried to capture the sight on camera. But on top of this mountain, I felt like we were on top of the world. Mountains in the distance didn't seem to even come close to the height of ours.

We spent about an hour on the summit, taking pictures and admiring the scene, before we had to head back down. One of the pictures taken was us as a group, making the hang-ten sign with our hands, and hanging our tongues out. We were also all wearing identical bandannas on our head that Madeline had given us for reaching the top. The picture is an awesome reminder of that afternoon on the summit. I doubt I'll ever be in a situation like that again.

I thought it would be a breeze for us hiking wise, but in reality, getting down that mountain was just as hard, and even at times harder than going up.

During the time going up, the Voices weren't that bad. Relatively bearable. But on the way down, my adrenaline got going because of my fear, and the Voices started kicking in full force. They were shouting that I was clumsy and I was going to fall to my death. I'd make a decision to try one route, and they'd yell at me that I was stupid and to try the other route.

It didn't take me long before I started to get confused. I was on the verge of bursting into tears. Their power over me was overwhelming.

When I finally conquered their hold on me by praying and focusing on the rocks I was climbing, the Voices tried another tactic.

"Jump!" they shouted. "Jump and be free! Be free of us forever! Just jump!"

That was almost a breaking point for me. Here I was on the top of a mountain of steep rocks, and I was being encouraged to "jump and be free!"

Trying to gain control back, and keep my feet planted safely on that mountain was an intense struggle. By struggle I mean not only did I have the Voices promising me *freedom* of them, which is what I wanted most, but I had to resist them. I had to resist mentally *and* physically.

Physically, my legs were ready to jump. I felt as if I wasn't in control of them anymore, that they could jump any second without me moving a muscle.

My mind could follow them, and rationalize that 'yes I could jump and be free', but it also figured out, 'I'd die'.

The two seemed so equally pleasing. I'd be free...but I'd be dead. It seemed the *only* way to actually be free *was* to die! That was worth it wasn't it? After all I did believe there was a heaven and a loving God waiting for me.

That thought of God started a new battle in my head. Now the Voices were telling me I was from Satan. I was actually the Devil! I was possessed! And the only way to free me from that, was, you guessed it, to jump.

Of course! That made sense to me now. Jump, to be free from Satan... Jump to be free of the Voices... Jump and die... but now be free to go to heaven.

It was a nightmare. Here I was, trapped on a mountain summit, struggling with Voices, thinking I was possessed, knowing I was crazy and belonged in a looney bin... And the saddest part was, *I couldn't tell anybody. I was all alone. These guys had become my best friends. The instructors were equipped for anything, but not this…. and I couldn't tell a soul. I had to bear this weight on my shoulders, and life, all alone.*

I don't know how I got off that mountain. But I do know one thing for sure. God was with me that day on that mountain. He wasn't going to leave me there. He helped me safely down.

I have found myself on many 'mountains' since then. But God has always been there. He is a faithful Father to me, and He will never forsake me.

The next big day we had was repelling a large introverted rock face named 'Devil's Punch Bowl'. It was at least 15 stories high, probably even higher. First we had to hike up the back way to the top, and then the instructors had to rig up the ropes. So it was quite a while just waiting at the top, occasionally looking down over the cliff to satisfy our curiosity and challenge our fear.

Finally we each got to repel down, hanging suspended in mid air, having only an old used rope keeping us from death. It was quite exciting. The experience was a little scary to say the least, but still a once in a lifetime opportunity. Once again, a challenging experience brought the members of PASD-056 a little closer to each other.

After that big thrill, our next planned event was going to be 'Solitude'. It consisted of three days of solitude at a site picked out by the instructors. We were prohibited from leaving the site and trying to seek out the others. We were to stay in our areas with our packs and sleeping bag and the small bag of trail mix and a few Bickies. One of the instructors would bring us a hot meal in the evening, but besides that, we had to ration our food.

Laurie picked out my site, and as she was taking me to it, she told me I had a really great spot, the best one. It felt good inside that she had taken such an interest in me, and seemed to like me. When we got there and I scoped it out, I was very satisfied. I knew I could get comfortable there.

However, when she started to leave, I became very anxious. I asked her to stay for a few more minutes, and she did. I was really worried about being alone for three days. I was afraid I would get confused and wander off or start hallucinating. Of course I couldn't tell her that, but I wanted to. But once she left and the Solitude started, I laid out my sleeping bag and fell asleep.

I slept for most of the 72 hours. There were a couple times that I was very tempted to search and find my buddies, but I didn't want to ruin it for anyone that was enjoying their time in solitude. As it turned out though I, the big rebel, known so well for breaking rules, was the only one that spent the whole three days alone. Everyone else was either found, or found others.

Even Laurie didn't seem to believe me when she came with my dinner on the second night. She looked at me suspiciously and asked me if I'd been with any of the other guys. I assured her I hadn't, but it wasn't until we all got back together as a group that she was convinced I hadn't lied. It hurt a little, but only because it was a reminder of who everyone thought I was. A troublemaker, liar, punk... the list went on

After we were done with Solitude, we moved into 'Finals'. Finals was the test to see if we had what it takes to survive now. We were going to be split up into smaller group, which made me pretty anxious. Would I still have Laurie as an instructor? Would I know anyone in the new group? Would my new peers accept me?

Well, somehow us girls convinced Laurie to try and get us an all girl group. She said it wasn't probable, but as long as there was a chance, we had to push it. We lucked out. We got a group of just girls, keeping all the PASD-056 girls together, and adding two others from another group.

Madeline was still one of our instructors, but Marvin and Laurie had been replaced with another female instructor. Since it was Finals, the students had to navigate and cook all on our own. So we needed a leader, and I volunteered.

We didn't really talk about needing someone in charge, but I could tell that the girls were a little intimidated by the idea of being on our own. Therefore, I knew they would be relieved if I took charge of things.

Finals were to last five days, and on the last day, we'd hook up with the rest of the students. Then we would run a 10K, and upon crossing the finish line, we would see our parents for the first time in 24 days. But first we had to get through the five days.

That afternoon, Madeline gave me the destination for the following day. I scoped it out on the map and we were off. We had the rare pleasure of hiking down a trail that day, and a few miles down we would make a left turn onto an adjoining trail.

I was having such a great time hiking along down this easy trail, that I missed the turn completely. None of the girls noticed it, and Madeline and our new instructor were so deep into conversation, they didn't notice either. Of course had they noticed, they weren't supposed to tell us anyway, cause we were on our own.

When we came upon a good-sized field, I knew that I'd screwed up. I got out the map, but while I was trying to focus on it, the Voices were distracting me with all their comments… "You're completely lost! You're all lost! You're going to all starve and die you idiot! You don't know what you're doing!"

Fighting back the tears from the embarrassment of the Voices, and the worried looks on the faces of my friends, I pushed all my energy into studying the map. It really wasn't a big deal. Obviously we had just missed the turn, and had to hike back to it. The only serious question was how far. Still, with the Voices in my head, just this small overstep was a huge problem.

I stuffed the map back in my pocket, and told the girls we would have to back track. They didn't seem concerned at all, and even the instructors joked about how they had missed it also.

We headed back down the trail and hiked almost three miles before we saw the turn. Now was the hard part. According to the map, it was a steep trail, and it would be at least five miles before we would get to where I'd planned out that we'd camp for the night. However, it was only an hour before dusk, and once it got dark, navigation would be much more difficult. Besides that, our bodies would be hungry and tired.

So the pace that I set was a little stronger than we were all used to. A couple of the girls complained, but still kept up. I think they knew that it could be them that was in charge, and that was a big responsibility. One they weren't ready for.

About two and a half miles up, after hiking in the dark for 20 minutes, I decided we'd stop. I came upon a small clearing, and thought since there were only seven of us, we could sleep there. We took a vote and it was unanimous. Tired and hungry, we dumped our packs and plopped to the ground.

Before we had started our Finals exhibition, we were given food to choose from. I saw some macaroni noodles and a huge block of cheese. I grabbed it, knowing that I could make some mac'n'cheese for dinner, and then we'd have left over cheese to put on our Bickies for a snack.

So that night I fixed a great dinner that everyone loved. Even the instructors were impressed. That was when I knew I'd won everyone's approval. Even the Voices in my head couldn't argue with the food. It was good!

The next day we had a little extra hiking to do to make up for the day before, but with that high carbohydrate meal in our system, we made good time.

Over the next few days, we hiked more miles, and did some rock climbing as well. It was very fun navigating, except for when the Voices would try to get me confused.

The last day of Finals was bittersweet. It was exciting that we were going to see our parents again, but the thought of leaving the mountain lifestyle and our new friends was sad.

When we were hiking that last day, we ran into a group of guys, some of them from our old PASD-056 group. It was great to see the guys again. Having an all girls group was cool, but we were also attached to the guys.

We hooked together and shared stories as we hiked our last miles to civilization. When we came across a street, an actually paved road, I became very excited. I jumped off the four-foot high bank onto the street and knelt down and kissed the asphalt. My pack fell over onto my head, pushing my face into the street. I was a little embarrassed, but I knew that this moment would stick in my memory forever. It had been 24 days since we'd walked on a street, let alone saw one.

The instructors herded us over to the next to last Base Camp, and we unpacked our stuff. We turned in all that was theirs, and put our personal stuff in a box to be given to us later.

Then they sent us on a 10K run. At the end of this run, all on asphalt fortunately, we would hit the finish line and see our parents. I used to be a runner, and only attempted one real 10K race when I was twelve, and I had wanted to make it under an hour. But I didn't. Since then, I hadn't attempted entering in a long race, for fear I would once again fail.

But that morning, I felt like I was flying, I was running so fast. The Voices were there as usual, but the harder I ran, the easier it was to push them out of my head. My adrenaline was racing, and I felt so good. I felt like I was on top of the world. I felt so good about myself, realizing what I had accomplished the past three plus weeks. I knew that with a map and a compass, you could drop me anywhere on that map in the mountains, and I could not only survive, but I could find my way out. That felt good. My self-esteem was at its highest ever.

As I approached the end of the run, and I could hear adults cheering up the hill around the corner, and I knew my parents were there waiting. I really got excited.

Imagine that. A troubled adolescent on the verge of turning eighteen in a few days, harboring a mental illness, scared of my parents through most of my teenage years, who now I couldn't wait to see.

Outward Bound had changed my life. When I turned that corner, and I saw my parents, I saw something in their eyes I hadn't seen in a long time. I saw HOPE and I saw PRIDE. They finally had hope that things were going to change for them and for me. They also had pride in their eyes. And I could almost read their minds, thinking to themselves as they looked at me, "That's *my* daughter. *Our* daughter. The one with the beaming smile on her face. The one that looks very happy and satisfied and proud of herself. That's our girl! The one we knew could do it.

I started sprinting as soon as I saw them, and ran straight into their arms. We all embraced, choking back tears, savoring the moment.

This was why they had sent me. This was what the Outward Bound School was all about. It had served its purpose, and its lessons would stay with me forever. I was taught more about self-esteem, friendships, and love for one another in those 24 days, than in my entire life.

The righteous cry out and the Lord hears them from all their troubles. The Lord is close to the brokenhearted and saves those who are crushed in spirit. Psalm 37:17-18

Chapter Twenty-Six

The Delusions

linda

It had been a month since Andrea showed up at my apartment bleeding. Very little had been said about her leg. She wore long pants until it healed up. I could sense that the episode was very embarrassing for her. I saw that as a good sign. When I first met her, she seemed oblivious to her bizarre behavior. I now realize that many of the traumatic episodes we experienced together left her with little memory. I, however, was aging a lot faster than I wanted to. To this day, I blame her for the gray hairs that I now have.

"Boss, do you think I did this to my legs?" She was looking at one of her old scars.

"Yes, not intentionally though. I believe you did it while hallucinating."

"I think so too."

That was the end of the discussion. I didn't want to push her. I knew that the sorting out of her delusions had to be done during her own time frame. I did not want to rush it; I wanted her to be ready to discuss her delusions when she was comfortable. I tried to put myself in her place and tried to imagine someone telling me that what I believe was true, wasn't. What if a friend told me that my father had not died eleven years ago? That the funeral I remember attending never happened.

How unstable would that be to me? What if I was told that I could not rely on my brain to tell me the truth?

It was another two months before Andrea opened the conversations again about her scars. She brought it up one day, and I knew she was ready to talk about it. It was still very difficult for her. She struggled tremendously. She admitted that her delusions about Craig raping her and the cuts being a result of him were embarrassing for her. I reassured her that the delusions about Craig and the drugs were all a part of her illness. She was an innocent victim of the chemical imbalance in her head. I reminded her of who she is and whom she belonged to. God has had His hand on her life prior to her conception. He knew she would be adopted into the Nelson family and He knew that she would be afflicted with schizophrenia. Yet, he allowed the disease because He knew she could handle it. Her purpose in life was to glorify her Lord. As long as she glorified her Creator, nothing about her life should she be embarrassed about, or apologize for. Her value was not based on her illness, but whom she is…a child of God created in His own image.

Andrea is very complicated, yet simple. She copes with ugly visual hallucinations, yet is frightened when someone sits next to her on the bus. She is shy, yet I've seen her reach out to a stranger in need. She can be introverted, yet sit down and write music lyrics straight from her heart. I have watched her at the piano as her creativity flows from her brain down to her finger tips, and yet I have seen her get frustrated because she can't remember how to tie her shoes. She also is very sensitive to what is going on around her. She hears things and sees things that I miss. We will be taking a walk and she will spot a Blue Jay perched upon a nearby tree. We will be walking through the mall and she will hear one of Amy Grant's songs being softly played over the intercom system in a near by store. She remembers a sermon our Pastor gave months ago, while I struggle to remember if I went to church on Sunday.

andrea

I recall Boss asking Dr. Connors during one of our sessions if I would eventually be able to sort out my delusions. With a look of sadness he nodded and said "most likely not." That was the day I made a commitment to myself that I was going to prove him wrong.

Learn to do right! Seek justice; encourage the oppressed.
Isaiah 1:17

Chapter Twenty-Seven

The Welfare Office

linda

Because Andrea was on CMS, County Medical Funding, we were told that she would have to apply for Medi-Cal, which is state funded. I called the welfare office and made an appointment for 7:30 a.m. I knew it was a waste of time because in order to be eligible for Medi-Cal you had to be under eighteen, elderly, pregnant, or disabled. She obviously was not the first three and the fourth had not been determined yet. But the County Medical Services insisted that we go through the application process. Later I learned that even though she would not get medical funding, she was eligible for food stamps.

    It was close, but we were going to make it. As I drove into the parking lot I glanced at my car clock. It was 7:28. We both quickly walked into the office and approached the window. The waiting room already had about seven people seated. As I stood at the small window I could see two older women employees. They looked at me briefly and continued to talk to each other. As I cleared my throat, one of the women turned and came over to the window.

    "May I help you?" She said in a manner that told me she really didn't want to.

"Yes, I am Linda Edmunds, and I am here with Andrea Nelson. She has a 7:30 appointment."

The woman looked right at me and stated, "You are late, you missed your appointment."

I looked up at the large clock displayed behind her and saw that the clock said 7:32.

"Excuse me, It is only two minutes past the time, and I have been standing here at least three minutes if not more."

"Sorry ma'am, you will have to make another appointment."

Andrea had come up beside me at the window. I was always conscious of her inability to cope with confrontation, so I was hoping she would have stayed in her seat.

"I have taken a day off of work. I do not live in this area. I left my house at 6:15 in order to get here this morning and I do not want to make another appointment. I was not that late."

I didn't yell, but I was firm.

"You are welcome to come back at 10:00. We might have an opening then."

I was so mad, I just glared at her, hoping she read my body language. It was obvious that she was not going to budge.

"I'll be back!"

Andrea and I left. Since neither of us had eaten any breakfast, we decided to find a place to eat.

We were back in the Welfare Office at 9:30. I did not want to take any chances of missing my second appointment for the day. I was handed a questionnaire to complete. When I was done, I looked around the room and sadness came over me that eventually turned into anger. I realized that the treatment I received was customary. The lack of warmth was evident as I watch the staff interact with the others. In the chair beside me was a mother with an infant and a small child. Across from me was a young couple with a child that had some special needs. I watched as they were directed to fill out the forms, sit, wait and don't ask any questions. Most of them in the room looked beaten by life circumstances. I am sure for many asking the government for assistance was their last resort. A tall woman came out from a door and called Andrea's name.

When we stood, without a smile she told us to follow her down the hallway to room six. Room six was a small closet like room that had two chairs placed in front of a glass window. There was just enough space between the small shelf and glass to pass papers underneath. At eye level was a small opening where the lady on the other side would communicate.

Again we were greeted without a smile. Worst than that, the woman looked at the papers and asked which one of us was Andrea Nelson, without looking up.

"Good Morning, how are you today?" I said, attempting to muster up some cheer.

The caseworker looked at me surprised and with a slight smile said, "Fine".

Andrea was shyly answering the questions that were being asked. At the same time a print out was coming off of the printer next to the caseworker.

She placed in front of her. "I see that during the year 1998 you earned $14,000."

Andrea and I looked at each other and giggled.

"Ma'am, Andrea was only employed during the month of January and February of that year. There is no way she could have earned that amount of money in two months."

"But this is what the records show." She said as if to challenge me to disagree with the records.

All of a sudden Andrea leaned over and said, "Boss that is not my social security number. She was pointing to the print out.

"Excuse me, the social security number does not belong to my friend."

"Yes it does!"

Andrea looked at me puzzled. "Boss, that is not my Social Security number, look at it."

I was straining my eyes to see the small numbers on the page. I was never good at reading upside down."

"Ma'am, Andrea says that is not her Social Security number."

The women looked at the print out and replied, "Yes it is, there is no mistake, it says Andrea K. Nelson."

Andrea was looking at me in bewilderment. One thing I knew, Andrea had a keen mind for numbers. She remembers phone numbers, addresses, dates and anything that has to do with numbers. Andrea even knew my Social Security number, after seeing it only once. I knew Andrea was right.

"It might very well say Andrea K. Nelson, but I guarantee you, that is not her Social Security Number. Possibly there is another Andrea K. Nelson."

Quickly the case worker shot back, "It has her birth date. Is she not twenty-eight years old, born on August 31th?!"

Andrea shot another look at me, "Boss the eighth number is not correct."

"Ma'am, the eighth number is not correct."

I could tell that the caseworker was irritated. As she passed a piece of paper under the glass, she asked Andrea to write down her social security number.

The caseworker started typing on her keyboard. Within seconds another printout was made. Both Andrea and I were watching her carefully as the case worker walked over to her printer behind her. I knew there was an error, but I also knew that if it was not clarified in the next few minutes it would take months for the government to correct the mistake. And as long as they thought Andrea could generate that kind of income, we had a big problem.

The caseworker was studying the piece of paper. She finally looked up at us and said, this is quite unusual, but there are two Andrea K. Nelsons, same age, same birthdays, only difference is one digit in the social security number.

Both Andrea and I were not only relieved, but had a tinge of self-righteous satisfaction that the caseworker had been proven wrong.

The caseworkers said food stamps were available, but she needed to ask some additional questions. "Who pays for your food currently?"

Andrea answered sheepishly, "She does." as she pointed towards me.

"Do you live with her?"

"No."

"Do you sit down and eat at the same time as the people you are living with?"

"No."

"Who pays for your clothing?"

By this time Andrea had been asked way too many questions. The questions were starting to unnerve her. I could tell that she hadn't quite recouped from the last confrontation relating to the Social Security Number.

Quietly she said, "No one."

"Who bought the clothes you have on".

Andrea looked down at what she was wearing. I also took a quick glance. She had on jeans, that were oversized for her small frame, a T-shirt, with a faded collar that peeked out from a very worn out sweatshirt, that had holes down the sleeve .

Very impatiently the woman said, "Someone must have bought the clothes you have on."

"Come on, I said half irritated and half humorous, "Does it look like these clothes were just bought at Nordstrom?!"

Realizing that sarcasm was not helping the situation, I tried to clarify.

"The clothes she has on were most likely purchased years ago, or given to her.

Once that process of the interview was over, we were asked to go back in the waiting room. We were instructed to stay for a video that was shown every half hour. The video was to be shown in room 501. We were told that they close the doors exactly on the hour and if we were late we would have to wait for the next showing. I looked at my watch and it was 10:55. I motioned to Andrea to get moving. I did not want to hang around for an hour. Right next to the room was a bathroom. I told Andrea that I would be right back.

I had just unbuttoned my pants and sat down when I heard Andrea open the door and yell, "Boss, come on, they are starting."

I told her to go ahead, I was right behind her. I quickly did what I needed to do and washed my hands. The door to 501 was closed. I did not see Andrea so I assumed she went inside. A sign was hung that said "IN SESSION DO NOT KNOCK". As I tried to open the door it was locked. I was sure the notice on the door did not pertain to me, so I knocked. I knocked again a little harder. I knew Andrea was in there alone and probably freaking out. Finally a woman in her late twenties opened the door.

"The session has started, you can not come in."

"Excuse me, it is only 10:59 according to my watch. My daughter is in there and she should not be in there alone."

The woman rolled her eyes and let me in.

The room was the size of a small classroom. I went and sat down next to Andrea, who looked very relieved that I was allowed in.

Looking around I noticed only five other people in the room.

The "instructor", for lack of a better word, made a few comments regarding the importance of keeping the Welfare Office abreast of any changes in employment, income, or change in address. She then turned on the video and sat at her desk facing the classroom.

The video started. It was explaining the Welfare system and what was expected of the recipients.

I leaned over after about five minutes into the film and whispered to Andrea, "How long?"

Andrea took her hands out of her pocket and indicated fifteen minutes with her fingers. No sooner had she done that the instructor stopped the video, got up from behind the desk and came across the room to where we were seated. Everything was quiet with the exception of the clicking of her heals on the linoleum floor.

"You will have to leave." She then turned around and went to the door and held it open for me to pass through. I was flabbergasted. I couldn't for the life of me figure out how she heard me from across the room, whisper to Andrea, two words...'how long?'

"You got to be kidding?"

"No I am not. You can wait outside in the hallway until this session is over. You will be allowed in for the next session.

I was not about to argue with her in front of the other five people, so Andrea and I went out in the hall and sat on the bench.

We both looked at each other a little unnerved.

"Boss, you got us kicked out."

Just then the two of us started cracking up. We laughed at the vision of the instructor, with her high heels, marching across the room to scold me.

"I'm sorry sweetheart."

"Boss, I can't believe you got us kicked out. She told us that we could not talk, that is why I gave you hand signals."

"I'm sorry. I didn't know we weren't allowed to talk. I was whispering very softly."

Andrea and I remained on "detention" for the next fifteen minutes. Once the last person left the room, the instructor, tapped her high heels over to where we were waiting and stated that we may go in. She obviously was going to give us a private showing.

As soon as the two of us sat down, she started the video. About three minutes into it I looked at Andrea to make sure she was ok. I gave her a quick smile.

"That's it! I will have to separate you two," said the instructor as she was pointing for me to move to the opposite side of the room.

This was beyond ridiculous. I moved over to where she was pointing without any comment, because I was scared at what might come out of my mouth. She started the video again. During the video she would look up every once in a while to make sure we were behaving.

When the video was over, I immediately stood up.

"I need to go over a few things with you", said the high heel tappin' instructor.

I looked over at Andrea and could tell she was not doing well. All the commotion was taking its toll on her.

Just then the high heel tappin' instructor looked over at her and asked her if she was ok.

By now Andrea had her legs up on the seat, curled up into a ball.

"No," I replied, she is not. You have upset both her and me and she is going to have a seizure!"

That comment obviously unnerved the instructor, which was my intention. Andrea looked over at me and I gave her the look as if to say, "Go ahead kiddo, have a seizure, this would be a good time."

The instructor got up from her desk and offered Andrea a banana. Andrea would not even look at her. I personally wasn't sure whether to laugh or get angry. What the heck was this woman thinking? She just spent the last 40 minutes harassing us and now she offers Andrea a banana as a peace offering. Go figure!

We will give ourselves continually to prayer, and to the ministry of the word. Acts 6:4

Chapter Twenty-Eight

The Bribe

linda

Well, I thought life as I knew it with Andrea, was going to get easier, now that she was on meds. She would take the meds and be well. WRONG. Things just got more complicated. First, the medication was expensive. A thirty-day supply cost around $400. Then she hated the way she felt. She said she felt tired and drugged. She said the voices were telling her to flush the medication down the toilet; that the medicine was poison. I was getting frustrated. I was in tears constantly. I would call her to see if she took her medication and she would say, "I can't remember." One time she said she thought she took it twice that evening. On top of all that, she was still having symptoms. Not as severe, but nonetheless, enough to discourage both of us. We both had high expectations.

I was afraid she was going to get discouraged and stop taking her medication all together. I needed a plan, something to motivate her. Andrea talked often of the time when she was in such great physical shape because she would get around on a bike.

I told Andrea I had a plan. I was going to buy myself a bike. I would take her with me and she could pick out the bike for me. I would then give her the bike to use for as long as she took her medicine. If after six months she were faithful to take her medication, the bike would become hers. If at anytime during the next six months she stopped taking her medication I would take the bike back and she would not have another chance at ownership. I made it clear that I would sell the bike in order to recoup some of my expenses. I made it very official. I drew up a contract and on June 12th both of us signed the agreement. If she were compliant with her medication, this awesome mountain bike would be hers on December 12th. After that time if she decided not to continue her meds, the only consequence would be she would have to live with her symptoms.

I had read that some of the side effects, such as drowsiness and the drugged feeling, usually went away after three to four weeks. I also had a feeling that if I could get her to take her medication for six months that she would see the difference in her life, and realize the benefits outweighed the side effects. She had lived in a world of voices, visual hallucinations, and frightening bodily sensations for almost eleven years. As frightening as her experiences were, it had become a way of life; it was the only thing she knew. She needed a taste of what it would be like to have a quiet mind.

Her family and the Leonard's were rightfully concerned about her biking around town, but I knew we had to give her some freedom. By this time she felt as if she was a prisoner in (as she would put it), "in the blue room, in the house on top of the mountain."

It had been seven months since I called the Leonard's and asked if she could stay with them until I found a place for her. I felt it was important to keep Andrea's morale up. She was struggling with more than any of us could ever imagine. At times she would talk about wanting to die. I couldn't blame her. She was twenty-seven years old, and in the world's eyes, without much hope for a successful future. I knew God had a plan for her, and I prayed that someday it would be made clear to her.

My prayer life took on a whole new meaning during this time. I would call every morning around 9:00 a.m. to check on how her night went and what plans she had for the day. Almost every day she had a bike trip planned. All bike rides however would eventually lead to me. But during her route she would go into shops and browse. A few times she went to the library, which I encouraged. Once she was done doing her own thing she would bike to the transit center, put her bike on the bus and come down and see me. I would of course take her out to dinner and bring her back up the mountain. She was having the time of her life with her new found freedom. Andrea having a bike overall was a good decision. It was building her self-confidence. She was exercising and getting fresh air instead of sitting in her rocker with earphones on, listening to music. Her appearance was improved. She was acquiring a beautiful golden tan that was envied by all.

I do recall a day that caused me to rethink my decision. She called me at work and said she was in San Marcos. This was not the plan that we had discussed earlier that morning.

"Hey, Boss, Uh..h..I think I got a little confused."

"Where are you?"

"I am in San Marcos."

"I thought you were going to ride your bike to your mom's in Escondido."

"Ha, that was the plan, but somehow I must have gotten confused. I was having such a good time riding my bike and before I knew it...I was in San Marcos, near the UPS where I used to work. I guess my brain remembered that I used to ride my bike to work, and when I saw the road I would take to work, I just turned onto it. As you would say Boss; I guess I zigged when I should have zagged."

Andrea managed to get her bearings and found her way back home without any further occurrences. However, when the Leonard's got wind of her detour that day, they were not happy with her or me for giving her the bike.

Be imitators of God, therefore, as dearly loved children and live a life of love, just as Christ loved us and gave Himself up for us… Ephesians 5:1-2

Chapter Twenty-Nine

The SSI Denial

linda

As soon as I was able to make a copy of the disability form that Dr. Connors had completed, I sent it in with the other government forms. Now all we had to do was wait. I was warned that it took about five to six months to get a reply back. I told Andrea that we would most likely not hear anything until mid summer.

It had only been about five weeks when I received the letter from the Social Security Office. I was surprised that they had responded so quickly. I tore the envelope open in anticipation. I was shocked. The request had been denied. As I stared at the letter and re-read the first paragraph hoping that I had read it incorrectly, I felt the tears well up in my eyes. As I read further, the letter stated that the seizures were not a disabling illness. I then realized that in my rush to get the application out I had forgotten to change the diagnosis at the top of the front page from seizure disorder to schizophrenia. The Social Security Office obviously did not look beyond the front page. If they had they would have seen the physicians statement and see the diagnosis that Dr. Connors had written down.

Tom and I agreed that we needed to appeal right away. I wanted to make sure the second request wasn't going to be denied so I went for overkill. I approached her mom and asked if she would write a brief letter explaining Andrea's odd behaviors since a child. I went to the Leonards and asked both Arnold and Pamela to write a letter documenting what they had experienced with Andrea over the years. I also wrote a letter explaining what I had witnessed the last eight months. I included every ER chart note I had requested. I had highlighted words and statements that I wanted to draw attention to. I made copies of a few of Andrea's letters to me, and those she wrote during her high school years. All revealed bizarre behavior. I also included some "scary" pictures that she had drawn which clearly showed signs of thought disorder.

By the time I was through, even a child would have recognized a severe mental problem. The envelope was three inches thick. I literally inundated them with data.

That night on the phone I did not tell Andrea about the denial. I wanted to tell her in person. My plans were to head up the mountain over the weekend.

The next morning Tom was taking me to work. He was done with law school and had applied for a job in Perris, California. He was anticipating an offer within the next few days.

"Are you going to see Andie tonight Hon?"

"Yes."

"How do you think she will react to the denial?"

"She will be very disappointed. Without money coming in, she feels dependent on the Leonards for a roof over her head."

If I get the job in Perris, we will find a three bedroom place and she can come live with us.

I could hardly believe my ears. I was almost speechless. I said *almost speechless,* because I did say something very stupid and trivial considering the content of our conversation.

"She has a cat."

Tom looked at me with a smile, "I know."

"Sweetheart, you amaze me."

Looking back on it today, I can see God's hand at work. God knew that if it were Tom's idea, my family and friends would have more respect for the decision. Tom is known as a man of God who is open to God's leading in his life. I, on the other hand have a history of jumping into things and praying about it later.

That evening Andrea and I worked all night on a project that we had started together. She and I were making a *wedding mailbox* for my son's wedding. It was something that we could do together. It gave Andrea a sense of accomplishment. I, not being very crafty, spent most of the time watching and cheering her on as her creative juices flowed.

It was getting late and I needed to head home. As I would routinely do, I called Tom to let him know I was about to leave. He asked me if I had told Andrea that she could live with us.

"I haven't said anything yet. I haven't even told her about the denial."

"Tell her now."

"Sweetheart, are you sure about this? Maybe we should pray about it for a while."

"Linda, I have prayed about it. Unless you have strong reservations, I think it is what we should do. Tell her now while I am on the phone."

Andrea had gone to the bathroom to get ready for bed. As I met her in her bedroom with the phone in my hand, I said, "Andie, I have disappointing news and hopefully good news for you. Social Security denied your disability. I will have to appeal. Tom is on the phone and he wants me to tell you that we are going to be looking for a place to live in the next month or two and we want you to help us find a place and move in with us."

Andie stood there dumbfounded as if she wasn't sure she heard me right. I repeated myself again. I could hear Tom through the phone asking me, "What did you say? What did she say?"

"Well sweetheart, she looks like she doesn't believe what I said. But wait… she is starting to smile, that's a good sign. Hey I think she likes the idea. Oh no, she is starting to cry. Maybe she doesn't like the idea. Wait…she is giving me a smile through her tears. Honey, I think it's a plan."

If I say, "My foot slips", Your mercy, O Lord, will hold me up. In the multitude of my anxieties within me Your comforts delight my soul. Psalm 94:18-19

Chapter Thirty

The Gun

linda

In just one week Andrea was going to be moving out of the Leonard's and into a condo with Tom and I. We were all excited.

Andrea and I had spent the day bike riding and were both exhausted. She wanted to sit in her chair and rock. I wanted to lie down and not move. After a quick nap of thirty minutes I was refreshed enough for the drive home.

I had put on my left tennis shoe and was looking for the right. I was looking down between the dresser and the bed figuring it had slipped under the bed. The bed was so high off the ground I had to get off the bed and crouch down. The space between the dresser and Andrea's bed was very narrow. I put my hand between the mattress and box spring for balance as I felt around under the bed for my shoe.

I found my shoe, but that was not all; my right hand that I was using to balance myself had found something also. Lifting up the mattress slightly I could see the rifle.

Oh my gosh, so Andrea was not bluffing. She did have a gun. A few minutes before my discovery Andrea had gone upstairs to get something to drink. I quickly took the serial numbers off the butt of the rifle and wrote it down. I was not sure why I felt I needed to identify the gun; there was no doubt in my mind that it belonged to Arnold.

I was curious to what Andrea was going to do when we moved. Would she just leave it between the mattresses or would she put it back. I would know next week.

In the meantime I would keep quiet. As much as it unnerved me that she really did have a rifle, I was confident that it was not loaded. Andrea had to have had the gun under the mattress for the last nine months. I didn't think it would cause a problem in the next five days.

And we know that all things work together for good to them that love God. Romans 8:28

Chapter Thirty-One

The Move

linda

Change is usually a challenge for most people, but to a paranoid schizophrenic, change is overwhelming. As much as Andrea wanted to live with us, she was scared. Although she was now on medication, she still would get confused and wander. If she were in a place that wasn't familiar to her she would leave and start wandering until something looked familiar.

Our move-in day was a Thursday, so the plan was that I would take a few days off work and move Andrea and me in prior to the weekend. Tom would move in on the weekend, along with our furniture.

The morning of the move Andrea seemed delighted and excited. Andrea had very little to move. She had a rocker, T.V., a dresser, her bike and some boxes of clothes and toys. I had borrowed my son's truck and the two of us were going to pack it up and get settled in before the day was over. I had purchased a bed for her and it was to be delivered that afternoon.

It did not take us long to pack up the truck. We had pulled the truck around the back of the house up to the door of the blue room. Every once in a while Arnold would come out and look over the balcony and take a peek at what we were doing.

I could tell he was struggling with two emotions…*'glad to see you movin on'*, and *'I am going to miss you.'*

Well, the truck was packed. The bedroom and bathroom were clean, leaving only one more thing to do. Get Gus the cat. At least that was what Andrea thought was all that was left to do.

"Sweetheart, you have something you need to take care of before you leave."

"What?"

"You need to return something you took of Arnold's."

Andrea gave me an odd look as if to say, "Okay".

A few minutes later she came running out and was ready to jump in the truck.

"Andrea, did you give the gun back?"

"Yeah, I put it back," she said without looking at me.

"Andrea, I didn't want you to *put* the gun back, I want you to *give* the gun back."

"Why?"

"Andrea, I want you to go back upstairs and tell Arnold that you took his gun and apologize."

Andrea put her head down and asked if she had to. I insisted. Slowly she went into the house. When she came out I could tell that she was relieved the issue of the gun was behind her.

"Let's get out of here," she said with her cat in her arms.

The day of the move went well. We celebrated by getting take-out and eating on the floor of the empty living room. As evening was approaching I could see that she was getting anxious. I myself was anxious, as I lay down. I already knew the problems Andrea had trying to sleep, and staying asleep, so I was prepared for little sleep myself that night. I was so tired from the move, yet I didn't want to fall into a deep sleep and not be there for Andrea if she needed me.

Sure enough, during the night she got up and I heard her walking around. As I came into the hallway, I could see her trying to open the front door.

"Honey, where are you going?"

I could tell she was confused. It was as if she were sleepwalking. I led her back to bed and lay down beside her with one eye open all night. The next night she tried to leave again. So once again I slept with one eye open.

The weekend was hectic, but once Tom and I got all our belongings in the condo, I felt better. I purchased a Christmas bell and hung it on the doorknob of the front door. Each night at least once I would wake up with the jingle as Andrea was attempting to leave. That first week, on the way home from work, Tom purchased two chains for the front door, one placed at the top of the door and the other at the bottom. Then he bought an alarm that would sound if the door actually opened and someone walked through it. Tom and I were afraid she would feel embarrassed and hurt. On the contrary, Andrea seemed relieved and pleased that we had gone through the effort to keep her safe.

For the next two weeks I was routinely awakened by the sound of Andrea trying to open the door. She literally was pulling the hinges off the doorframe. In her confusion she would be unable to remember the chains and would yank at the door, unable to figure out what was keeping the door from opening. I was always able to wake up and get to her before she caused too much damage. I was relieved that she couldn't figure out the chains. If she did, the alarm would have gone off. I wasn't sure how I would explain the commotion to the neighbors. We laughed about what we would say if someone complained. I thought of what explanation I would give. Tom reminded me that the alarm goes off when someone enters also, so we could claim it was a burglar alarm.

Fortunately the alarm never went off. After about six months we stopped setting the alarm and even forgot it was there, until a few weeks ago. The complex we live in was recently sold. The new owners were going through all the condos to check for needed repairs. Andrea was home alone the afternoon the inspectors came to our place. After she let them in, she noticed the three men looking at the alarm and all the chains in bewilderment. One of the men looked at Andrea, but before he could say anything, she smiled, and made a flippant comment.

"What can I say? My parents are not only getting old, but paranoid."

Direct my steps by your word, and let no iniquity have dominion over me. Psalm 119:133

Chapter Thirty-Two

The Wanderer

linda

One Saturday afternoon I had fallen asleep on the couch. Tom woke me up and said Andrea had left and had been gone over twenty minutes. Andrea had ceased wandering in the middle of the night and we assumed that she had gotten used to her surroundings and wandering was no longer going to be a problem. Beside this was the middle of the day. I ran outside immediately. She was nowhere in the complex to be found.

"Tom, you stay by the phone, just in case she calls. I'm getting in my car and searching the neighborhood."

I had gone around the block twice. If she had been gone over twenty-minutes she could be miles from here. Dusk was setting in and I was frantic by this time. My mother bear protective instincts kicked in. The thought of her wandering around aimlessly, scared and confused broke my heart. I had to find her before dark, "Ok God, I need some guidance. Which direction should I start looking?"

The first thought that came to my mind was to go to the main street in our neighborhood that led to the freeway. It was a busy commercial area. I went about three miles and then turned around so I could look on the other side of the street. No sooner had I made my U-turn when I saw Andrea sitting on a small retaining wall with her head down resting with her hands holding her head. As I stopped the car and got out, I called her name. She didn't even look up.

"Andie, I have been looking all over for you. Andie!"

She slowly looked up at me as if to say, "Are you talking to me?"

At that moment, I realized she didn't recognize me. "Andie, it's Boss, let me take you home."

I spent the next five minutes coaching her into my car. She was reluctant at first, but came with me as a child would with a stranger. I was confident that once we got home and she saw her bedroom and all her belongings, she would snap out of her catatonic state. I was wrong. She sat on the bed terrified. Her cat came in the room and she leaned over and petted him as if she was seeing him for the first time. I asked her if this was her cat and she nodded her head no. I asked her a number of other questions including how old she was. She whispered seventeen. After asking a few more simple questions, I realized Andrea had no recollection of anything past that age. She seemed tired so I suggested she lay down and take a nap. She very reluctantly laid down and immediately feel asleep. She did not wake up until morning. She slept until 9:00 a.m.

I could hear her opening her door and heading to her bathroom. I met her in the hallway not knowing what to expect.

"Hi Boss. Why are you looking at me that way?"

"Good morning sweetheart, I was just coming to see if you want to join me for breakfast."

"Sure."

She obviously was clear headed and did not recall last night. It was about two days before I decided to talk to her about it. I knew that she would be upset and I needed to approach the episode gently. She didn't remember leaving. The last thing she remembered was sitting in her rocker listening to music. I faxed her psychiatrist a description of what took place. He called me and suggested I increase her medication, which I did.

A few weeks later it happened again. This time we were heading out to do some shopping. When I got to the bottom of our stairs outside I realized I had forgotten my sunglasses. I told Andrea I would be right back. When I came back Andrea was not in sight. I saw some kids playing on the grass and I asked them if they saw which way Andrea had gone. They pointed in the opposite direction from where my car was parked. After looking around for a few minutes, I decided to get in my car and head out toward the street. I had only gone about three blocks when I spotted Andrea walking down the sidewalk. I honked and pulled up beside her and rolled my window down.

"Hey there, need a ride."

Andrea looked at me strangely and nodded her head no, as she continued to walk.

"Where are you headed?" I said without letting her know I was concerned.

She stopped and looked at me with a blank expression.

"Would you like me to take you home?"

She nodded yes. I then got out of the car and opened the passenger side door for her. She got in, still without any expression.

"Do you know who I am?"

She nodded yes.

"Good, let's go home."

As I drove into our complex I could see that she was looking relieved. By the time she got in her room I could tell that her head was clearing. Needless to say, we never made it to the grocery store that night. By the morning the whole incident was a memory to me, and a fog to her.

I was fairly convinced that her lapse of memory and confusion had everything to do with schizophrenia, and not a neurological problem as her psychiatrist suggested. Andrea reminded me that she had lost time since in high school. I also read on the label of her medication, that even though it was rare, one of the side effects of the mediation was confusion. In either case, whatever the cause, Andrea was a wanderer and I in turn was a nervous wreck.

...Because His compassions fail not. They are new every morning; Great is Your faithfulness. Lamentations 3:22

Chapter Thirty-Three

The Treatment Center

linda

Her psychiatrists recommended Andrea attend a local Day Treatment Center. The Center is designed to assist those with a mental illness. Daily workshops are offered in the areas of, symptom management, coping skills, socialization, behavior modification, medication updates, and many other topics to help the mentally ill get back into the mainstream of life. In order to get into the program, a psychiatrist must refer you.

As soon as I got in the car, after her twenty-minute session with her psychiatrist, my thoughts were racing. The whole concept of Andrea attending a day treatment program thrilled me. This is just what she needed. She would learn all that I had discovered about her illness. She would be able to make friends with others that she could relate to, and could relate to her. She would have at her disposal professionals that could council her on a daily basis.

I couldn't wait to get home and make the phone call that would put her on the waiting list. Well, like always, I was a little ahead of the game. Looking over at Andrea sitting on the passenger side of the car, I could tell that her thoughts were racing also, but in a very different direction than mind.

"You look deep in thought Andie. Are you thinking about the day treatment program?"

I heard a weak, "Yeah."

"You look concerned."

"I don't want to go."

"Why, I think it would be great. You will learn about your illness, which will help you understand yourself, and therefore learn skills in order to cope."

"What if I am unable to concentrate? I won't learn anything."

"Andie, you will be with others that struggle with the same issues you struggle with."

"I don't want to be around other mentally ill people. It will be too depressing. Besides I am not a people person. I don't make friends easily."

"Andie, trust me, this will be good for you. You will have counselors that will get to know you and work with you."

"Yeah, and they could commit me to a mental hospital."

"Sweetheart, please don't be so negative. Let's put this item at the top of our prayer list. Okay?"

Andrea reluctantly agreed. I insisted that Andrea put her name on the list reassuring her that being on the list did not commit her to anything. When I called, I was told that there was a three to four month wait. I welcomed the time figuring I would need it in order to convince Andrea of the wonderful opportunity being offered.

The only mention of the day treatment program was during our prayer time when I would ask God for guidance.

It wasn't more than a week and I received the call at work from Kenesis, the day treatment program. They had an opening and wanted to schedule an interview with Andrea. I went ahead and made the appointment figuring I could always cancel if I couldn't get Andrea to agree to go.

"Hey Andie, guess what?"

I figured if I acted up beat and excited, she would automatically get on the same page as me.

"I got a call from the day treatment center. Can you believe that they already called and that they have an opening? This must be God, huh?"

Well, not only did I not get the excited response that I had hoped for, I got nothing.

"Andie, are you there?"

"Andie!"

"Andie, answer me."

"What."

"Okay, tell me what that head of yours is thinking."

"Do I have to go?"

"Yes, but keep in mind, you are interviewing them also. We might not like the program. Just because we go for the interview doesn't mean you are making a commitment. Come on Andie. I'll take the afternoon off. We will go together, and then go to lunch and talk about it."

I finally convinced her.

The place looked clean and impressive. My excitement went a higher level. The first thing on the agenda was the tour. I think they do that in order to get the "clients", (the term they use for those that attend the Center), to relax and get familiar with the surroundings. The first room we visited was the Art Room. A large room with banquet tables placed together in the middle of the room. Next was the library, which included along with books, a number of computers, and a T.V. with a VCR. Around the periphery of the room were some worn out couches. The café was located directly next door to the Recreation Room, which displayed a well used pool table. I estimated that the café would seat about fifty people. The room was well lighted by the sun, and displayed very simple, childlike artwork on the walls. The actual kitchen facilities were very accommodating. (Little did I know that one day, Andrea and I would have some great memories cooking and serving together in that very kitchen.). As we went upstairs we were shown a number of small rooms in which "groups" were held. At that point I was already to get my checkbook out and sign on the dotted line.

On the Road to Peace

Alice, the director brought us into her office and introduced us to Amy. Both women were going to interview Andrea. Prior to arriving, Andrea and I had the conversation regarding me staying with her the whole time. I said I would if she felt she needed me to.

The first thing we needed to do was fill out a two-page questionnaire. They both left the room while we worked on the form. I could see Andrea was getting anxious just looking over all the questions.

"What if I answer wrong?"

"Andie, this is not a test. There is no right or wrong answer. This is an assessment of your needs. Come on, let's go over each question together." Once we finished, I went to get the two women.

As soon as they walked back into the room, I could feel Andrea tense up. I looked at her and gave her that look that said... ANDREA... RELAX... YOU ARE WINDING YOURSELF UP!

Both Alice and Amy were very pleasant and kind. They wanted to go over the questionnaire. Alice started out with some of the benign questions and answers, such as, where in Escondido do you live and is it near a bus line. Andrea was doing well with her answers, even though she would not look at either woman in the eye. She kept her head down and sheepishly answered the questions. Then the hard part. Alice started to question her about the "voices" and what they tell her to do. Do they ever tell her to hurt herself or others. Very quietly, Andrea said,

"I don't talk about what the voices say."

This was very true. She rarely would even tell me what the voices were telling her.

Just then Andrea looked at me. I could read her eyes. She was scared and wanted me to jump in and rescue her. The ladies, however, read something else into it. They thought that she didn't want to say what the voices would say in front of me, so they asked if I would mind stepping out.

Andrea immediately got agitated and said, "There isn't anything I can't say in front of Boss." I put my hand on her shoulder to let her know that everything was all right.

"Andie, please answer the question. I will be right outside the door."

It was hardly two minutes, when Amy poked her head out and said I could come in.

"Andrea claims that the voices have told her to hurt others, but she says she never obeys them," said one of the counselors.

"That's correct. She has never hurt anyone in her life, and I am confident she won't."

"Well," Alice said very firmly, "As we told Andrea, we will not tolerate any physical violence."

On the drive home Andrea was very quiet. As soon as we walked in the door, Andrea blurted out. "Boss, they don't want me at the Center because they think I am going to hurt someone."

"Andie, relax, they need to ask those questions to everyone."

"They think I didn't want to answer because you were in the room."

"I know."

"I just don't like to talk about the voices."

"I know that too."

Andrea was accepted. Amy was assigned to be her counselor, which Andrea liked since she had already met her during the interview process. Kenesis requested she attend at least three days a week. She decided to go Monday, Wednesday, and Thursday. The first week was nerve-racking. She called me about every half-hour to say she wanted to go home. Of course, I encouraged her to stay. Bribing worked well with Andrea, so I promised dinner at her favorite fast food restaurant, Taco Bell, as soon as I got home from work.

The second week was a little better, and by the third week, she seemed to be accepting the program. She discovered that on Fridays they had outings, so she decided to change her attendance days to Monday, Wednesday, and Friday.

Just as I thought things were going great and Andrea was adjusting, things changed. She started calling me from home saying she left Kinesis early, or Amy, her counselor, would call and ask why Andrea did not show up. I would call home and she would say she wasn't feeling well so she decided to stay home. I could see a pattern. After a few weeks of these excuses I asked her what was really going on. She finally told me that she was hallucinating more than usual and it seems to be happening during the day while at Kenesis.

"Well, I think that is a perfect place to be if you are hallucinating. You are with people who understand. Just tell Amy, your counselor that you are hallucinating. Andie, that is what she is there for."

We must have talked for at least fifteen minutes when the truth came out.

"Sheri, my friend at Kinesis said that if you are hallucinating, they will take you to the hospital. I don't want to go to the hospital."

"Andie, I don't believe that statement is true."

"I don't want them to know I am hallucinating."

I told Andrea that I would call Amy the next day and find out about the policy. My understanding was that if the counselor felt Andrea needed medical care, I would first be contacted. After talking to Amy, it was verified that my understanding was correct. I shared my information with Andrea and reminded her that she carried a cell phone in which she could call me anytime of the day if she felt threatened, but most importantly, Kinesis knows to call me if any situation warrants medical care. Andrea reluctantly went back to the treatment center.

The first day Andrea and I went for the interview at Kinesis we were told about the Jubilee Ringers. It was a group that played the bells and chimes, directed by Penny. I made a mental note that day that I would encourage Andrea to join. With her musical talents, I thought this would not only be fun for her, but an asset to the group. It wasn't more than a month after attending Kinesis that Andrea became one of the ringers. She came home excited about her decision.

Penny had made an impression on Andrea and Andrea really liked her. Penny is a warm Scottish woman, in her late sixties, who has a son suffering from schizophrenia. Even though her son no longer attends Kinesis, Penny has been volunteering her time for the last ten years. She makes the forty-five minute drive from her home every Monday morning, bringing with her all the bells and chimes, for an hour practice. Throughout the year she arranges concerts. During the Christmas season she organizes visits to a number of nursing homes in the area. Most of the Ringers do not drive, so arranging for ten people to get from point A to point B, is not always easy.

The highlight was when they played this year at the NAMI (National Alliance for the Mentally Ill) Convention in San Diego. Tom and I, along with her family attended. Andrea and the Ringers were all very nervous, but they did extremely well. Penny had bought them all red shirts with the logo *Jubilee Ringers* in gold printed on them. Each one purchased tan pants, which made them all look very professional. I was so proud of the group that day. Performing for a crowd is usually difficult for most, but when you have a mental illness it can be formidable.

Andrea never missed a practice, once joining the Ringers. Even during the couple weeks she started leaving and going home hallucinating, she always managed to stay until after the Ringers practice on Monday morning. Four months into the program Andrea started enjoying the interaction with her new friends, and to this day, attends Monday through Friday. I believe that the drawing point was her involvement with Penny and the Ringers. I have told Penny time and time again that her ministry has truly made a difference in Andrea's life.

In the eighteen months that Andrea has been attending the day treatment center, counselors have come and gone with the exception of the one that was assigned to Andrea. God knew that Andrea did not like change; therefore was faithful to take care of the smallest detail, such as arranging for her to be hooked up with the one counselor that would assure her stability for the next two years.

...and that every tongue should confess that Jesus Christ is Lord... Philippians 2:11

Chapter Thirty-Four

The Insight

linda

Andrea's strong suit in dealing so well with her illness is her capacity for insight. She has made an effort to understand her illness. She now recognizes her symptoms and makes the necessary adjustments. When things start getting distorted, or the voices become loud she tries to do something to relax, such as listen to music. If she is home, she will go to her room. If she is out, she will head home.

Andrea has a cute "Spiderman" cap that I became familiar with early on in our relationship. She had it with her at all times. I noticed a pattern; just before she was about to have a seizure, or become psychotic, she would put the cap on. She also wore it to bed. I realized there was some significance to her putting on the cap. Today she wears it very infrequently; however, when I do see her put it on, it is a sign to me that things are going on in her head. Andrea has such a great sense of humor; the other night as I walked up to her bathroom door, I caught her as she was putting the cap on.

"Hi Sweetie, did you take your medicine yet?"

"No", she said with a smirk, as she adjusted the cap on her head, "but I think it's time."

Finally, all of you, live in harmony with one another; be sympathetic, love as brothers, be compassionate and humble. I Peter 3:8

Chapter Thirty-Five

The Stigma

linda

The picture of the tortured soul, who dresses bizarre and wanders the streets, talking to himself, is the exception, not the norm. Today, an estimated 2.5 million Americans are diagnosed with Schizophrenia. Because the disease carries such a profound stigma, those that are high functioning live secret lives, revealing their psychiatric problems only to their closet friends and family members.

Lack of knowledge, ignorance and compassion has enforced many of the myths attached to the disease. The stigma is real, and so is the misconception. Mental illness is an illness and not a weakness. It is not a character disorder or spiritual disorder. Having schizophrenia is no more a sin than having cancer. People with mental illness are not demon-possessed or victims of bad parenting.

I am now tuned in to the issue. It is not uncommon to listen to the news of violence by a person known to have schizophrenia. Of course they forget to mention that the person had been drinking for days and/or was high on drugs. Studies have shown that less than 3 percent of those with mental illness have the potential for violence, yet 80 percent of those depicted on prime time television are presented as violent. Often while watching television, for the sake of comedy, I hear someone referred to as being a *lunatic* or *psycho*. Any type of comedy at the expense of those that truly suffer is wrong. I just finished a book series by two well-known Christian authors that referred to someone in the book as *wacko* because the character was rocking back and forth in the fetal position after a traumatic event.

The truth is that most people with schizophrenia are usually less violent than others. Matter fact, they are usually very withdrawn and timid, and more likely to hurt themselves than others. They like to keep to themselves. They know that they are vulnerable, so they hide in fear. You are more likely to be attacked by someone who has been drinking in a bar than someone who is mentally ill.

I started immediately educating my children. I explained that Andrea had a brain disease that distorted her thoughts, and perceptions. Mental illness was not a lifestyle that she chose. She had done nothing wrong. It wasn't related to drug use or alcohol. She could not snap out of it if she wanted. No amount of therapy was going to change the chemical imbalance in her brain. It is complex, and debilitating, but not the end of her life. Andrea like anyone else deserved to be treated with respect, love and kindness as the rest of us.

It did not take long for my children to embrace Andrea as part of our family. They knew the scripture that says, "We are created in God's image," applied to her too. Sadly I found that this was not going to be the case with everyone. I found it interesting that there were those that had no religious background, yet very accepting, and then there were those that were raised in the church and taught of God's grace and love, were not very accepting. As one of my daughters so eloquently stated, "Mom, those that have made judgment, have obviously based it on ignorance, and they are the ones we need to feel sorry for. They obviously do not understand God's Grace and Mercy. We on the other hand, not only understand God's Grace and Mercy, but we are blessed to experience it through the life of a person sweet as Andie."

What my daughter said was true. Andrea's presence is a reminder to us that God cares about every aspect of our lives. We see His work in her everyday. Andrea also has shown us how to rejoice in all things. Many times I have seen her struggling with her symptoms and sneak off to her room to be alone. Within minutes, I can hear her, through the closed door, singing praise songs to the Lord…

I'm trading my sorrows
I'm trading my shame
I'm laying them down
For the joy of the Lord
I'm trading my sickness
I'm trading my pain
I'm laying them down
For the joy of the Lord

Let us not give up meeting together, as some are in the habit of doing, but let us encourage one another- and all the more as you see the Day approaching. Hebrews:10:25

Chapter Thirty-Six

The Richness

linda

When Andrea came to live with us, there were two things that we requested; she always take her medication, and she attends church.

We attend a large church and Tom and I knew the crowds were going to cause some amount of anxiety for Andrea. The first few months Tom and I prayed throughout the whole service that God would keep her head clear and her mind relaxed and quiet. I promised Andrea each Sunday on the way to church that if things started happening in her head during the service, I would walk out with her. During the first three months we had to leave the service only twice.

Now, almost two years later, not only has the anxiety of attending church disappeared, but she loves to go. She is the first one dressed and ready on Sunday morning. She has brought many and invited dozens to church. We now go in separate cars so she can pick up her friends.

Today is Mother's Day. As I sit holding Tom's hand, I glance down the row. I have all my children with me today: My two sons, my daughters, my daughter-in -laws, my son-in-law, and Andrea. And not too far from the sanctuary, in the nursery, is my first grandchild, Paige Elizabeth. Today Tom and I have very little in material possessions, but we have never felt richer.

We all have our daily struggles, but none compare to Andrea's. As the worship and singing starts, I look over at her as she holds back her tears and sings:

Open the eyes of my heart Lord
Open the eyes of my heart
I want to see you. I want to see you.
To see You high and lifted up
Shinning in the light of Your glory
Pour out Your power and love as we sing Holy, Holy, Holy

In Him we were also chosen, having been predestined according to the plan of Him who works out everything in conformity with the purpose of His will. Ephesians 1:11

Chapter Thirty-Seven

The Future

linda

What I have learned over the past eighteen months can never be taught in a classroom, or read in a book. My life will never be the same. Andrea has touched a part of my heart that had become stagnant. She has taught me to take time to watch a bird flutter from limb to limb, stop to pet a cat, slow down and listen to the music.

There is a lot of work to be done in Mental Health. Discrimination prohibiting adequate comprehensive health care and job opportunities must end. Research must move forward in finding new ways to not only treat, but also prevent Mental Illness. New opportunities in treatment and recovery must be implemented. But most importantly, we must have a change of heart; we must recognize the worth of every person, regardless of any disability and embrace the teaching of Christ...Love one another.

I would like to end our story with a poem.

My alarm goes off early as I wake to face the day
And before I start on anything I get down on my knees and pray
For today will be special, there's a lot to get done

On the Road to Peace

And only so many hours of the bright shinning sun
There is breakfast to fix for my large hungry family
Which today I'll enjoy and do very happily
Then the boys go to Little League and the girls to Ballet,
While my husband is busy heading down the highway
To his high executive job which has us living well
In our five bedroom house with the spiral stairwell
And there's the big green front lawn with the white picket fence
And of course with the back yard we spared no expense
There's a playhouse and the doghouse and the favorite tire swing
And the cute little bird feeder for the birds that sing
The pool is blue and warm all year long
In our home, we wanted to feel like we belong
There are pictures of us all scattered inside
And looking at my family I almost burst with pride
And speaking of them, they will all be home soon
And after some dinner, I'll tuck them in with the moon
And read them a story to help them tire
So I can go snuggle with my husband by the fire
And when it is time for me to turn in

I get back on my knees and with a prayer I begin
"Please God forgive me for acting this way"
Cause all that just happened was a make-believe day
I just wanted to forget I am mentally ill
And have all that I had, and even more still
But you helped me to realize that's not what I need
To experience some happiness I can't use greed
So no more make-believe, tomorrow I'll be true
Cause the life You have planned for me WILL glorify you

Written by:
Andrea Katherine Nelson
February 2001

Andrea currently resides in Georgia pursuing a career in Home Design and Renovation. (www.womenatworkforyou.com). She travels back to California two or three times a year to visit her parents, sister, and the woman she still fondly refers to as "Boss".

Linda and Andrea have shared their story of hope with audiences across the United States and Canada. You may contact them at lledmunds@gmail.com.

Breinigsville, PA USA
06 February 2011
254909BV00001B/107/P